THE GEOSTRATEGIC TRIAD

LIVING WITH CHINA, EUROPE, AND RUSSIA

Significant Issues Series
Timely books presenting current CSIS research and analysis of interest to the academic, business, government, and policy communities.
Managing editor: Roberta L. Howard

The **Center for Strategic and International Studies (CSIS)**, established in 1962, is a private, tax-exempt institution focusing on international public policy issues. Its research is nonpartisan and nonproprietary.

CSIS is dedicated to policy analysis and impact. It seeks to inform and shape selected policy decisions in government and the private sector to meet the increasingly complex and difficult global challenges that leaders will confront in this new century. It achieves this mission in four ways: by generating strategic analysis that is anticipatory and interdisciplinary; by convening policymakers and other influential parties to assess key issues; by building structures for policy action; and by developing leaders.

CSIS does not take specific public policy positions. Accordingly, all views, positions, and conclusions expressed in this publication should be understood to be solely those of the authors.

The CSIS Press
Center for Strategic and International Studies
1800 K Street, N.W., Washington, D.C. 20006
Telephone: (202) 887-0200   Fax: (202) 775-3199
E-mail: books@csis.org   Web site: http://www.csis.org/

THE GEOSTRATEGIC TRIAD

LIVING WITH CHINA, EUROPE, AND RUSSIA

ZBIGNIEW BRZEZINSKI

FOREWORD BY JOHN J. HAMRE

THE CSIS PRESS

Center for Strategic
and International Studies
Washington, D.C.

Copyright Acknowledgments
The publisher gratefully acknowledges permission to reprint the following:
"Living with China," *The National Interest* (Spring 2000); "Living with a New Europe," *The National Interest* (Summer 2000); "Living with Russia," *The National Interest* (Fall 2000). © National Affairs, Inc.

Photo Credits
Great Wall of China (p. xii). © Brian Vikander/CORBIS
Berlin Wall (p. 28). © Reuters NewMedia Inc./CORBIS
Kremlin Wall (p. 54). © Reuters NewMedia Inc./CORBIS

Significant Issues Series, Volume 23, Number 1
© 2001 by Center for Strategic and International Studies
Washington, D.C. 20006
All rights reserved
Printed on recycled paper in the United States of America
Cover design by Robert L. Wiser

2009   Sixth printing

ISSN 0736-7136
ISBN 0-89206-384-X

Library of Congress Cataloging-in-Publication Data
Brzezinski, Zbigniew, 1928–
    The geostrategic triad: living with China, Europe, and Russia / Zbigniew Brzezinski ; foreword by John J. Hamre.
      p.cm. — (Significant issues series, ISSN 0736-7136 ; v. 23, no.1)
    Includes bibliographical references.
    ISBN 0-89206-384-X
    1. United States—Foreign relations—China. 2. China—Foreign relations—United States. 3. United States—Foreign relations—Europe. 4. Europe—Foreign relations—United States. 5. United States—Foreign relations—Russia (Federation) 6. Russia (Federation)—Foreign relations—United States. 7. United States—Foreign relations—1989–
    I. Title. II. Series.
E183.8.C5 B75 2000
327.73051—dc21   00-012681

CONTENTS

FOREWORD   VII

1 LIVING WITH CHINA   1

2 LIVING WITH A NEW EUROPE   29

3 LIVING WITH RUSSIA   55

GEOPOLITICAL REALITIES   74

STRATEGIC PRIORITIES   75

ABOUT THE AUTHOR

FOREWORD

How should the United States define its international engagement with the rest of the world? More than a decade after the abrupt collapse of the Soviet Union, and more than a decade after the renunciation of authoritarian political systems and statist economic policies in key developing countries, a national consensus on how the United States as "hyperpower" should navigate in the world is as elusive as ever.

How can we explain the irony that the United States, at the moment of uncontested geostrategic preponderance, has no comprehensive basis for engaging the rest of the world?

There are a number of reasons. First, much of the public debate on American international engagement is cast in iconic terms that may satisfy embedded political interests but do little for positioning the United States to capitalize on a dynamic global environment. In the post–Cold War period, the critical issues have become increasingly complex. New challenges have been superimposed on traditional issues. A constellation of global forces is calling long-standing sovereign prerogatives and capabilities into question. All this defies bumper-sticker articulation.

Second, the absence of a broad consensus has provided a greater opportunity for special interest groups to impose their priorities on the policymaking process. The result is a centrifugal process that cuts into the capacity of leaders to formulate and carry out balanced and consistent policies.

Third, in the context of today's real-time news culture, political leaders are confronted with making complicated decisions based on a multitude of factors in ever shorter time frames. The "CNN effect" makes crises across the world immediately relevant to leaders who in the past would not have been affected by those developments. The pressure for instant policy declarations and formulation has grown tremendously. As a consequence, leaders have less time to think carefully about longer-range trends, confer with knowledgeable individuals, and contemplate approaches that are longer term and integrated in nature.

Fourth, the organizational "stovepipe" phenomenon of specialized jurisdictions, competencies, and interests across the U.S. government (as well as other governments) is creating increasingly segmented analyses of developments across the world. It is also generating turf battles and gridlock, infighting and paralysis, and lack of constancy of purpose. The constraints created by these organizational rigidities certainly apply to the range of traditional national security and foreign policy issues confronting the United States. But they are most pronounced when it comes to crosscutting global issues such as globalization, proliferation of weapons of mass destruction, HIV/AIDS and the cross-border movement of other infectious diseases, and other similar forces.

Fifth and last, the debate in both academia and the public policy community on how to position the United States relative to the rest of the world has been no more productive. Despite Herculean attempts to identify paradigms for U.S. engagement within a broader strategic framework, no overarching theory has emerged, no comprehensive strategy has succeeded in attracting political consensus, and no approach has enabled the systematic prioritization of American interests and objectives.

Together, these five elements have limited the capacity of leaders to think in "strategic" terms—to assess relations with key states in a comprehensive fashion, weigh both primary and derivative effects of proposed policies, cast relations in a long-term time frame, and develop an integrated approach to how Washington can and should define its relations with the world. The challenge is clear: American leaders must weigh all dimensions of complex relationships, assign priorities to highly complex and sometimes competing objectives, and fashion a strategy through which those priorities can be achieved.

For these reasons, Zbigniew Brzezinski's unique geopolitical insight is all the more valuable. Over the course of his remarkable career in government and the public policy arena, Dr. Brzezinski has consistently distinguished himself as a truly strategic thinker by grounding his analysis in historical understanding, exploring how sets of relations between countries can and should be calibrated with other sets of relationships, advancing conclusions that are global in scope, and focusing on longer-range developments and trends. In addition, he has consistently attacked the questionable assumptions and iconic thinking that have characterized public debate on some of the big issues of our times.

Dr. Brzezinski's analysis is testament to the fact that even in today's real-time decisionmaking environment, it is possible to formulate and prosecute a strategy based on a forward-looking, interdisciplinary approach.

This monograph captures such an approach. The conceptual staging point for the analysis that follows is that the success of U.S. international engagement in the early twenty-first century will be conditioned largely by the United States' relations with Eurasia—the world's central arena of world affairs—and in particular with China, Japan, Russia, and Europe. In short, Dr. Brzezinski asserts, the United States needs a well-defined transcontinental strategy to maneuver effectively in the twenty-first century. More specifically, he points to two "Eurasian power triangles" that Washington must develop as an organizing structure for its future engagement: the first between the United States and the European Union and Russia, and the second between the United States and Japan and China.

This monograph lays out Dr. Brzezinski's thinking on the considerations that should underlie each of these power triangles. For obvious reasons, each of these relationships involves separate and independent considerations. But they also share an important characteristic: Of the two countries other than the United States in each triangle, only one recognizes its stake in international stability. In the United States–Japan–China triangle, Tokyo clearly is pursuing regional and international policies that reflect an interest in security. Beijing, however, continues to favor more or less drastic alternations in the geopolitical calculus. The same applies to Russia in the context of the United States–European Union–Russia triangle. The European Union, conversely, serves with the United States as the axis of global stability. Also significant, as Dr. Brzezinski notes, is the important contrast between the two "non-stake" countries in the respective triangles. Beijing's economic progress suggests an altogether different set of priorities than the dire challenges—ranging from economic to health and demographic—facing Moscow.

In managing these differing sets of relationships, the challenge to Washington is to fashion a longer-range vision of its interests and role in Eurasia. That implies, of course, an outward-based strategy building on relations with our allies in Europe and Japan. In this context, a number of looming policy issues—NATO expansion, European integration, the development of an autonomous European defense capacity, the balance between Washington, Tokyo, and Beijing, cross-Strait relations—are likely over time to test traditional security, political, and economic relations. A longer-range vision also implies detailed and differentiated strategies for dealing with Russia and China.

What makes Dr. Brzezinski's analysis so significant is the clear and comprehensive conceptual road map he offers to address these issues. With these essays, he has articulated a strategy for the cornerstone of U.S. policy—our relations with Eurasia—as we move forward into the millennium. In so doing he has made a significant contribution at a significant time, and CSIS is pleased and proud to be able to publish this volume.

The three chapters that make up this volume were first published in successive issues of the *National Interest*, and we thank its editor, Owen Harries, who is also a senior associate at CSIS, for permitting us to incorporate those separate articles into a single volume.

JOHN J. HAMRE
President and CEO, CSIS
January 2001

CHAPTER ONE

LIVING WITH CHINA

Eurasian politics have replaced European politics as the central arena of world affairs. Once European wars became evidently threatening to America, there was no choice for America but to inject itself into European politics in order to prevent new conflicts from erupting or a hostile European hegemony from emerging. Thus America's engagement in world affairs was precipitated during the twentieth century by European politics. Today, it is the interplay of several Eurasian powers that is critical to global stability. Accordingly, America's policy must be transcontinental in its design, with specific bilateral Eurasian relationships woven together into a strategically coherent whole.

It is in this larger Eurasian context that U.S.-China relations must be managed and their importance correctly assessed. Dealing with China should rank as one of Washington's four most important international relationships, alongside Europe, Japan, and Russia. The U.S.-China relationship is both consequential and catalytic, beyond its intrinsic bilateral importance. Unlike some other major bilateral relationships that are either particularly beneficial or threatening only to the parties directly involved (America and Mexico, for example), the U.S.-China relationship impacts significantly on the security and policies of other states, and it can affect the overall balance of power in Eurasia.

Reprinted with permission. "Living With China," *The National Interest* (Spring 2000).

More specifically, peace in Northeast and Southeast Asia remains dependent to a significant degree on the state of the U.S.-China relationship. That relationship also has enormous implications for U.S.-Japan relations and Japan's definition—for better or worse—of its political and military role in Asia. Last but not least, China's orientation is likely to influence the extent to which Russia eventually concludes that its national interests would best be served by a closer connection with an Atlanticist Europe; or whether it is tempted instead by some sort of an alliance with an anti-American China.

For China, it should be hastily added, the U.S.-China relationship is also of top-rank importance, alongside its relations with Japan, with Russia, and with India. In fact, for China the Beijing-Washington interaction is indisputably the most important of the four. It is central to China's future development and well-being. A breakdown in the relationship would prompt a dramatic decline in China's access to foreign capital and technology. Chinese leaders must carefully take into account that centrally decisive reality whenever they are tempted to pursue a more assertive policy on behalf of their national grievances (such as Taiwan) or more ambitious global aspirations (such as seeking to replace American "hegemony" with "multipolarity").

In essence, then, in the complex American-Chinese equation, Beijing should be prudent lest its larger ambitions collide with its more immediate interests, while Washington must be careful lest its strategic Eurasian interests are jeopardized by tactical missteps in its handling of China.

FOR HISTORICAL CLARITY

It follows that the United States, in defining its longer-term China policy and in responding to the more immediate policy dilemmas, must have a clearly formulated view of what China is, and is not. There is, unfortunately, enormous confusion in America on that very subject. Allegedly informed writings regarding China often tend to be quite muddled, occasionally even verging toward the hysterical extremes. As a result, the image of a malignant China as the inevitably anti-American great power of the 2020s competes in the American public discourse with glimpses of a benign China gently transformed by U.S. investors into an immense Hong Kong. Currently, there is no realistic consensus either among the public or in the Congress regarding China.

In recent years, inconsistency has also characterized the attitude of the U.S. government. It is unfortunately the case that the Clinton administration has been guilty of "vacillation and about-faces on China, often in response to popular and congressional pressure," that the President himself was "not willing to protect U.S.-China relations from tampering by Congress," and that "some in Congress would destroy the relationship if given the opportunity to do so."[1] The presidential mishandling in late spring 1999 of the World Trade Organization (WTO) negotiations with the Chinese and the persisting inclination of Congress to grandstand on the China issue validate that indictment.

In addition, public perception of China tends to be defined by spectacular symbols that allegedly encapsulate the essence of today's and tomorrow's China. Thus, for many Americans Tiananmen Square and Tibet have come to reflect the central reality of enduring communist oppression and of intensifying national chauvinism. For others, the Chinese economic "miracle," dramatized by the skyscrapers of Shanghai, and by China's growing free-market openness to the world through the Internet, travel, and foreign investment, symbolizes a transforming nation that is progressively shedding its communist veneer. Which China, then, is the real China, and with which China will America clash or cohabit in the years to come?

Having digested much of the available literature on Chinese political, economic, and military prospects, and having dealt with the Chinese for almost a quarter of a century, I believe that the point of departure toward an answer has to be the recognition of an obvious but fundamental reality: China is too big to be ignored, too old to be slighted, too weak to be appeased, and too ambitious to be taken for granted. A major and ancient civilization—encompassing 20 percent of the world's population organized in a historically unique continuity as a single nation-state, and driven simultaneously by a sense of national grievance over perceived (and, in many cases, real) humiliations over the last two centuries, but also by growing and even arrogant self-confidence—China is already a major regional player, though not strong enough to contest at this time either America's global primacy or even its preponderance in the Far Eastern region.

China's military strength, both current and likely over the next decade or so, will not be capable of posing a serious threat to the United States itself, unless China's leaders were to opt for national suicide.[2] The Chinese nuclear force has primarily a deterrent capability. The Chinese military build-up has been steady but neither massive nor rapid, nor technologically very impressive. It is also true, however, that China is capable of imposing on America unacceptable costs in the event that a local conflict in the Far East engages vital Chinese interests but only peripheral American ones. In this sense, China's military power is already regionally significant, and it is growing.

Nonetheless, unlike the former Soviet Union, the People's Republic of China (PRC) is not capable of posing a universal ideological challenge to the United States, especially as its communist system is increasingly evolving into oligarchical nationalist statism with inherently more limited international appeal. It is noteworthy that China is not involved in any significant international revolutionary activities, while its controversial arms exports are driven either by commercial or bilateral state interests. (As such, they are not very different from those of France or Israel, with the latter actually exporting weapons technology to China.)

Moreover, in recent years China's international conduct has been relatively restrained. China did not exercise its veto to halt un-sanctioned military actions against Iraq over Kuwait. Nor did it block the Security Council's approval of the international protectorate in Kosovo. It approved the deployment of UN peacekeepers in East Timor, and—unlike India in the case of Goa, or Indonesia when it seized East Timor—it peacefully re-acquired Hong Kong and more recently Macau. China also acted responsibly during the Asian financial crisis of 1998, for which it was internationally applauded. Last but not least, its current efforts to gain membership of the WTO, whatever the merits or demerits of China's negotiating stance, signal the PRC's growing interest in global multilateral cooperation.

Internal Contradictions

The picture becomes more mixed when the domestic scene in China is scrutinized and when current Chinese views of the United States are taken into account. China is basically unfinished business. Its communist revolution has run out of steam. Its post-communist reformation has been partially successful, particularly at the urban-industrial-commercial levels, but this has required major doctrinal concessions and compromises. The result is that the Chinese system is a hybrid, with strong residues of communist dogmatism in the industrial sectors and in the state bureaucracy coexisting uneasily with dynamic, capitalist entrepreneurship driven by foreign investment. China's future systemic orientation is thus yet to be fully defined, but it is already evident that the cohabitation within it of communism and commercialism is inherently contradictory.

The trajectories of China's economic change and of its political evolution are thus parting. At some point, the distance between them will become too wide to sustain. Something, then, will have to give. Moreover, the existing political elite—itself not so young—will soon be replaced by a generation that came to political maturity neither during the Great Leap Forward nor during the Cultural Revolution, both epiphenomena of communist doctrinal exuberance. The emerging political elite matured during Deng Xiaoping's pragmatic upheaval in the Chinese economy, and hence may be more inclined to correct the political trajectory of China's evolution, bringing it closer to the economic trajectory.

The issue of human rights is thus likely to become more acute as the political regime seeks one way or another to close the gap between itself and its evolving socioeconomic context. The constraints on personal political liberty, the denial of religious freedom, and the suppression of minorities—most notably in Tibet—cannot be sustained in a setting of growing social and economic pluralism. The recent efforts to suppress the Falun Gong movement testify to the regime's sense of ideological and political vulnerability. Accordingly, the issue of freedom is bound to become both more critical and more difficult for the existing regime to manage. Indeed, it is almost safe to predict that in the near future—probably within the coming decade—China will experience a serious political crisis.

In any case, whatever its political prospects, China will not be emerging as a global power in the foreseeable future. If that term is to have any real meaning, it must imply cutting-edge superiority of a truly global military capability, significant international financial and economic influence, a clear-cut technological lead, and an appealing social lifestyle—all of which must combine to create worldwide political clout. Even in the most unlikely circumstance of continued rapid economic growth, China will not be top-ranked in any of these domains for many decades to come. What is more, its backward and debilitated social infrastructure, combined with the per capita poverty of its enormous population, represents a staggering liability.

One should note here that some of the current scare-mongering regarding the alleged inevitability of China's emergence as a dominant world power is reminiscent of earlier hysteria regarding Japan's supposedly predestined ascendancy to superpower status. That hysteria was similarly driven by mechanical projections of economic growth rates, without taking into account other complex considerations or unexpected contingencies. The Japanese purchase of Rockefeller Plaza became at one point the symbol of the paranoiac, one-dimensional glimpse into Japan's future.

Be that as it may, China's unsettled domestic scene is likely to reinforce an inherently ambivalent and occasionally antagonistic attitude toward the United States. Though Chinese leaders recognize that they need a stable and even cooperative relationship with the United States if their country is to continue developing, China is no longer America's strategic partner against a threatening Soviet Union. It became so after the Shanghai breakthrough of 1972 and, even more so, after the normalization of relations in 1980, which dramatically transformed a three decade-long adversarial relationship into a decade of strategic cooperation.[3] Today, with the Soviet Union gone, China is neither America's adversary nor its strategic partner.[4] It could become an antagonist, however, if either China so chooses or America so prompts.

Accentuating the Negative

Currently, Chinese policy toward the United States is a combination of functional cooperation in areas of specific interest and of a generally adverse definition of America's world role.[5] The latter has prompted Chinese diplomatic initiatives designed to undercut U.S. global leadership. Chinese policy toward Russia is ostentatiously friendly on the rhetorical level, with frequent references to "a strategic partnership." Such is also the case (perhaps not surprisingly) with Sino-French relations, with both sides proclaiming (as, for example, during the October 1999 Paris summit between Presidents Chirac and Jiang) their passionate fidelity to the concept of global "multipolarity"—not a very subtle slam at the disliked American "hegemony."

Indeed, the word "hegemony" has become the favorite Chinese term for defining America's current world role. Chinese public pronouncements and professional journals that deal with international affairs regularly denounce the United States as an overreaching, dominant, arrogant and interventionist power, increasingly reliant on the use of force, and potentially tempted to intervene even in China's internal affairs.

The NATO action in Kosovo precipitated especially a massive outpouring of Chinese allegations that America has embraced the concept of interventionism at the expense of respect for traditional national sovereignty, with dire implications for China. As one alarmed Chinese expert put it:

> Suppose serious anti-Communist Party or anti-government domestic turbulence erupts in China, which cannot be quickly brought under control, and, at the same time, the international community commonly joins the anti-China stream. In this case, the hegemonists (perhaps jointly with their allied nations) could launch a military invasion of China.[6]

The above was neither an extreme nor an isolated assertion. Such charges have been accompanied by growing concern that the United

States is accelerating and intensifying its efforts to construct an anti-Chinese coalition in the Far East, embracing what is represented as a dangerously rearming Japan, South Korea and also Taiwan, a coalition "that resembles a small NATO of East Asia."[7] American, Japanese and South Korean discussions of possible collaboration against theater missile attacks have intensified these Chinese suspicions. Occasional American and Taiwanese press speculation that Taiwan might be included in such a collective effort has also further aggravated the Chinese, who see it as additional evidence that the United States is increasingly inclined to make permanent the current separation of Taiwan from China.

Perhaps the most striking example of the current Chinese inclination to stress the negative dimensions of the U.S.-China relationship is the attempt to provide a deeper intellectual or cultural rationalization for the seemingly intensifying antagonism. The Chinese-owned Hong Kong daily, *Ta Kung Pao*, published a major editorial entitled "On the Cultural Roots of Sino-U.S. Conflict" in September 1999, advancing the thesis that "the conflict between Chinese and American civilizations is at a deeper level one between sacred and secular lifestyles." Amazingly for a nominally communist regime, it is China that is said to represent the former: "Chinese civilization has always stressed an integration of heaven with man." This identity is said to contrast sharply with "the consumerist and hedonist mode of behavior that grew out of American Civilization," making Americans "look down on Oriental Civilization, holding that it is backward and ignorant." The policy inference that was drawn from the foregoing was stark: "in China-U.S. relations, it will be absolutely impossible to permanently resolve conflicts of political views in areas such as human rights, democracy, and freedom."[8]

To be sure, the foregoing views are in part instrumental, for they are also meant to serve the current Chinese efforts to put America on the ideological defensive. They do not define for Beijing the overall character of the U.S.-China relationship. Since China seeks to reduce the scope of America's global preponderance (and its resulting leverage on China), it needs some sort of a doctrinal legitimation for controlled antagonism; yet China also wants to retain for itself, for obvious reasons of domestic self-interest, the vital benefits of collaboration with America. Striking a balance between the two is not easy, especially given the fact that China's communist leaders have not found an effective substitute for their previous Marxist world-view. That central reality imposes a severe restraint on Chinese anti-American proclivities.

Hence, U.S.-China military links are being preserved, economic ties enhanced and political relations kept relatively congenial—even while "multipolarity" is hailed and "hegemony" condemned in joint declarations with Moscow, Paris and whoever else cares to join. The result is a confused amalgam, involving communist terminology and Chinese nationalist sentiments. That mishmash reflects the ambivalent position in which the Chinese leadership finds itself both at home and at large, given the unresolved ambiguities of Chinese domestic and foreign policy.

Doubtless, China's leaders, generally intelligent and hardheaded, sense that inherent ambiguity. They must realize that Paris, rhetoric aside, will not join in some fanciful Beijing-Moscow-Paris anti-American coalition. They have to know that Russia does not have much to offer to China, except perhaps some technologically not very advanced military equipment. Ultimately, they have to understand—and their conduct reflects that they do—that at this historical juncture the relationship with the United States is central to China's future. Outright hostility is simply not in China's interest.

The foregoing points toward a further observation. China today, in relationship to the wider international system, is neither the militarist Japan of the 1930s nor the ideologically and strategically threatening Soviet Union of the 1950s–70s. Though all analogies, by definition, are partially misleading, there are some important parallels between China's current situation and imperial Germany's circa 1890. At that time, German policy was in flux, while Germany itself was a rising power. Like today's China, Germany's ambitions were driven by a resentment of a perceived lack of recognition and respect (in the case of Germany, especially on the part of a haughty British Empire, and in the case of today's China, on the part of an arrogant America), by fears of encirclement by a confining and increasingly antagonistic coalition, by rising nationalistic ambitions on the part of its predominantly

What China Is and Is Not: A Decalogue

1. China is neither an international adversary nor a strategic partner of the United States, though it is hostile to perceived U.S. "hegemony."

2. China is not going to become a global power, though it is a regional power capable of asserting its national interests.

3. China is not a direct security threat to the United States.

4. China does not pose a global ideological challenge to the United States.

5. China is not regionally destabilizing and is in fact behaving internationally in a relatively responsible fashion.

6. China is neither totalitarian nor democratic politically but an oligarchic-bureaucratic dictatorship.

7. China is not in compliance with universal standards of human rights and of tolerance for minorities in places such as Tibet or Xinjiang.

8. China is evolving economically in a desirable direction.

9. China is not likely to avoid serious domestic political strains because commercial communism is an oxymoron.

10. China does not have a clear vision of its political evolution or of its international role.

young population, and by the resulting desire to precipitate a significant rearrangement in the global pecking order.

One will never know with any certainty whether the European war of 1914, a quarter of a century later, could have been avoided by wiser policy in the 1890s. Similarly, one cannot be certain about which direction China will head over the next quarter of a century. However, already at this stage it should be self-evident which prospect is to be avoided. For America, that requires a strategically clearheaded management of the sensitive issue of Taiwan and, even more so, of the longer range task of fitting China into a wider and more stable Eurasian equilibrium.

FOR STRATEGIC PROPORTIONALITY

The Taiwan Question

For America, Taiwan is a problem; China is the challenge. Taiwan complicates U.S.-China relations, but it is U.S.-China relations that will determine in large measure the degree of stability or instability in the Far East and, more generally, in Eurasia. Admittedly, how the Taiwan issue is handled will influence—and in some circumstances could even determine—the evolution of U.S.-China relations. But, except for its impact on those relations, the status of Taiwan itself is not a central international concern.

Still, it is important to take both history and strategy into account when addressing the sensitive and volatile issue of Taiwan's relationship with the mainland. That issue is a direct legacy of China's civil war. It is also an unresolved legacy, for Taiwan's separate existence reminds that neither side involved in the civil war succeeded in totally eliminating the other. Though one side won by gaining control over the mainland, and thus over the vast majority of the Chinese population, the losing side still preserved itself not only as a political entity but also as a potential political alternative, even though entrenched on a relatively small island inhabited by only 2 percent of China's people.

That Taiwan succeeded in preserving its independence from the side that emerged victorious in the Chinese civil war has been due mainly to the United States. America, though indirectly, continued to be involved in that war even after its termination on the mainland in 1949. It both protected and bolstered Taiwan. Episodic military clashes in the Taiwan Strait occurred until the de facto suspension of the civil war in the 1970s—a suspension attained by direct U.S.-China talks initiated under President Nixon and later formalized through the normalization of U.S.-China relations under President Carter.[9] The resulting arrangement was genuinely creative, for it enabled the winning side to acquiesce to the de facto partition of China as the transitional outcome of the civil war without accepting it as a permanent de jure reality.

That sensible accommodation was made possible by the acceptance on both sides of the intricate formula whereby (1) the United States acknowledged that in the view both of the mainland and of Taiwan there is only one China; and (2) the United States affirmed that it expects the issue of reunification to be resolved peacefully (and that U.S. national interest would be engaged if it should be otherwise); whereas (3) the Chinese reiterated that reunification is an internal Chinese matter, to be attained by whatever means China deems appropriate, though their preference is also for a peaceful resolution.

Once that hurdle had been traversed it followed that the officially recognized government of China had to be the one that governs 98 percent of the Chinese people. And it also followed that Taiwan could not be recognized as a separate "sovereign" state, though the United States could maintain practical and functional ties with it. Such ties were then formally legislated by the U.S. Congress in the "Taiwan Relations Act" of 1980, which regularized U.S. relations with Taiwan without defining it as a sovereign state. In effect, the outcome of the great bargain preserved the formal unity of China while practically respecting the current reality of a separate status for Taiwan.

That arrangement has proven to be a blessing for Taiwan, while simultaneously permitting the development of extensive U.S.-China ties. Taiwan's resulting prosperity hardly needs documenting. It has blossomed both as an economic miracle and as a democracy in the more secure setting of abated Sino-American tensions, of continued U.S.

arms sales, and of the openly proclaimed U.S. stake in a peaceful Taiwan Strait. Taiwan's success has also provided stunning and encouraging evidence for the proposition that democracy and Chinese culture are compatible, an example that has significant long-term implications for the future evolution of mainland China.

Taiwan has not only prospered economically and flowered politically but has become a respected and active participant in various international organizations. For example, it is a full member of the Asian Development Bank, APEC and the Central American Bank for Economic Integration, and is currently seeking access to the WTO. It maintains regular economic, technological and cultural ties with more than 140 states with which it does not have formal diplomatic relations.

An even more impressive testimonial to the benefits accruing from the U.S.-China normalization of relations has been the actual pacification of the Taiwan Strait. In contrast to the sporadic clashes that used to occur prior to normalization, there has been a massive flow of capital and people across the hitherto separating water.[10] These socioeconomic ties, in turn, have permitted the emergence of an informal but serious dialogue between representatives of the respective authorities.

Lee's Unilateralism

That informal accommodation was jeopardized in the second half of 1999 by the unilateral redefinition of Taiwan's relationship to the mainland, abruptly launched by the Taiwanese authorities. In a highly publicized interview, President Lee Teng-hui of Taiwan suddenly abandoned the "One China" formula, redefining the Taiwan-mainland relationship as involving "state-to-state relations." The import of the new formulation was self-evident: one China was brusquely redefined as two separate states. Moreover, Lee in a subsequent statement insisted that the inhabitants of Taiwan have acquired a "fresh national identity based on the New Taiwanese consciousness."[11]

Lee's initiative was launched without any prior consultations with the United States. It was immediately followed, however, by stepped-up efforts by Taiwanese supporters in the United States, encouraged by a well-financed Taiwan lobby, to induce the U.S. government, through congressional pressure, to take a stand in support of

Taiwanese "sovereignty."[12] Various supporters of Taiwan also launched a public campaign alleging a growing Chinese military threat to Taiwan, urging particularly the Republican presidential candidates to support the so-called "Taiwan Security Enhancement Act," introduced earlier in the year in the U.S. Congress. That proposed act aimed at nothing less than the de facto revival of the 1955 Mutual Defense Treaty with the Republic of China (terminated following the U.S. recognition of the People's Republic of China), with its specific and non-discretionary provisions designed to restore Taiwan as a U.S. military ally against China.

It should be noted that these alarmist pressure tactics disregarded the fact that the PRC currently lacks, and in the foreseeable future will not have, the airlift and sealift capability to effect a successful 120-mile, cross-strait amphibious invasion. One need only recall the enormous difficulty of the Normandy landings in 1944 across the narrower English channel, in spite of overwhelming allied air and naval supremacy as well as the relative weakness of the German forces. In contrast, the Taiwanese ground forces that would be resisting any landing communist forces are relatively better armed and more mobile. Taiwan also has the means to contest PRC efforts to assert air and naval superiority in the Taiwan Strait.

It is also noteworthy that the U.S. secretary of defense, in an assessment issued in February 1999, concluded that only "by 2005, the PLA [People's Liberation Army] will possess the capability to attack Taiwan with air and missile strikes which would degrade key military facilities and damage the island's economic infrastructure."[13] Even then, the acquisition of such a capability would not mean that the PRC could execute an effective invasion. One must also take into account Taiwan's capacity to retaliate effectively by striking or mining China's major ports, thereby cutting China's trade links with the entire world.

In any case, whatever may have been Mr. Lee's motives in publicly venting the formula of "state-to-state relations," there was no pressing security need for his unilateral initiative. Hence the question: cui bono? Since the Taiwanese leadership had to know that it would complicate U.S.-China relations and generate new tensions in the Taiwan

Strait, one has to assume that the initiative was taken (at least in part) on the calculation that any U.S.-China military confrontation, even if provoked by Taiwan, would work to Taiwan's political advantage.

For the United States, acquiescence to the new formulation and passage of the proposed "Taiwan Security Enhancement Act"[14] would mean that Taiwan has been granted nothing short of a carte blanche to redefine its status as it wishes, with the United States obligated to defend the island, come what may. It would amount to a de facto unconditional guarantee of U.S. protection for whatever provocative step Taiwan might take, including even a formal secession from China, and thus it would be a repudiation of prior U.S.-China undertakings. It is also important to note that in any ensuing hostilities in the Taiwan Strait, the United States would find itself altogether isolated internationally.

For China, the proposed U.S. legislation would signal America's reengagement in the Chinese civil war, while Beijing's acquiescence to the new "state-to-state" formulation would mean the formal acceptance of the permanent partition of China. Neither is a palatable choice for Beijing. It would also mean that, in the eyes of the Chinese, the grand bargain with the United States had been exploited by Washington, first to consolidate Taiwan, and then to transform a separatist Taiwan into a permanent U.S. protectorate. No current Chinese leader could accept such an outcome and normal relations between the United States and the PRC would thereby be jeopardized.

The Clinton administration was, therefore, fully justified in repudiating the new Taiwanese formula and in reassuring Beijing that previous U.S.-China understandings remained in force. For some time to come, Washington will have no choice but to navigate carefully between the risk inherent in any unconditional assurances to Taiwan's security and the obligation to discourage any Chinese attempt at coercive unification. Perhaps an additional bilateral Washington-Beijing clarification regarding Taiwan might be helpful if it were to involve a clear-cut Chinese commitment (expressed, naturally, as a unilateral Chinese decision) never to use force in order to achieve national unity, matched by a simultaneous—and similarly "independent"—U.S. commitment to terminate all arms sales to Taiwan if it should formally declare itself to have seceded from China. However, even then, the U.S.-China relationship would still remain vulnerable to disruption because of the unresolved and always sensitive issue of Taiwan's future. That is why it is unlikely that either side would be willing to exchange such mutual assurances.

Democracy: The Essential Condition

Ultimately, the issue of Taiwan will be determined primarily by what happens in China itself. A China that fails to evolve politically, or that flounders socially—not to speak of a China that regresses ideologically—will not attract Taiwan. Nor will it intimidate Taiwan, for the United States will continue to have a tangible national interest in the prevention of warfare in the Taiwan Strait. It follows that Taiwan will, and should, continue to have prudently measured access to the necessary U.S. military wherewithal for self-defense.

In contrast, a successfully developing and progressively democratizing China may eventually be able to reach some practical arrangement with Taiwan. It might do so by enlarging the "one country, two systems" formula (currently applied to Hong Kong) to "one country, several systems."

The "one country, two systems" formula was unveiled, with considerable publicity, by Deng Xiaoping during my meeting with him in Beijing in 1984. It was explicitly designed to accommodate Taiwan. In 1997, during a visit to Taiwan, I used the phrase "one country, several systems," having in mind—in addition to China—Hong Kong, Macau and perhaps eventually Taiwan. In an interview with the London *Times* (October 18, 1999), President Jiang tantalizingly observed, in speaking of "the main objectives for China *by the middle of the next century*," that, "We will ultimately resolve the question of Taiwan and accomplish the great cause of national reunification by adhering to the policy of '*peaceful reunification* and one country, two systems' after the successful return of Hong Kong and Macao." (The italicized passages [my emphasis] clearly hint at historical patience.)

At this stage, it is not possible to be more precise, but Taiwanese spokesmen are generally correct in postulating that China's democratization is the practical precondition for any arrangement that may approximate (and eventually become) reunification. It thus follows that the real strategic challenge for the United States—more important than the issue of Taiwan—pertains to China's evolution, both in its domestic politics and especially with regard to the global mindset of its ruling elite.

That evolution can be subtly influenced from the outside, even if a democratic transformation of China cannot be so imposed. Positive change in China will come, in the main, from socioeconomic pressures, unleashed (in part, unintentionally) by the ruling elite's otherwise rational economic reforms. Their cumulative effect, especially because of modern mass communications, is inherently incompatible with enduring political repression. In that context, the cause of human rights can be, and should be, deliberately supported from the outside, even at the cost of some friction with China's rulers.

China, however, is not America's client state. Nor does it pose a global ideological challenge like the former Soviet Union, in which case it was useful to put that country on the defensive by making human rights into a major issue. Indeed, a policy of sustained ideological confrontation with China is more likely to delay desired changes by stimulating more overt regressive reactions from an increasingly insecure political elite. Given the ongoing changes within China, including its evident trend toward more openness to the world, the promotion of human rights in the country is likely to be more effective if pursued with deliberate indirection.

For example, extensive programs to assist the Chinese in embracing the rule of law are bound to have a significant democratizing impact. Indeed, as the negative experience of post-Soviet Russia shows, loud emphasis on electoral democracy can prove to be self-deceptive. In contrast, the institutionalized spread of the rule of law can create enduring foundations for genuine democratization while enhancing the prospects for a functioning market economy. Since the ruling elite finds the latter to be in its interest, the propagation of the rule of law is both politically easier and in the long run more effective.

Similarly, the development of functional assistance to local officials, who in increasing numbers are subject to election, should be a major focus of an enlightened but not strident program on behalf of human rights. The stronger and more democratic the local government, the weaker the central controls. Yet here, too, the top political elite is susceptible to seductive co-optation since it realizes that an effective local government is necessary for successful modernization. Human rights can thus be piggy-backed onto China's own domestic ambitions. The U.S. Congress would be well advised to bear the above strictures in mind, while providing more support for various nongovernmental organizations engaged in helping the Chinese to develop a genuine civil society.

The matter of Tibet is more intractable, especially since a strategy of indirection is not responsive to the more immediate grievances of the Tibetan people. Hence, on this issue a public stance of disapproval is unavoidable. At some point, the Chinese government may conclude that the costs to China's reputation are too high, and that some creative application of the "one country, several systems" formula would provide a more constructive solution to what is clearly a major violation of established international norms for the treatment of ethnic minorities. Direct talks with the Dalai Lama would represent a significant step in the right direction, and continued U.S. support for the Tibetan people is thus in order.

The Japan Factor

Effective management of these delicate issues is more likely if the United States sustains a policy that progressively enhances the Chinese stake in a peaceful Northeast Asia and in a constructive Chinese role in a stable Eurasian power equilibrium. Only in that larger context can the salience of the Taiwan issue eventually be subsumed and the formula of a democratic and prosperous China as "one country with several systems" become reality. Moreover, just as the United States could not have conducted a successful policy toward the Soviet Union without simultaneously calibrating most carefully its relations with Europe, so American policy toward China must also be, almost by definition, a triangular policy, shaped with Japan very much in mind.

China is especially sensitive to anything pertaining to Japan and its changing international role. China views Japan both as a historic rival and as an extension of U.S. power. The character and scope of the U.S.-Japan alliance is hence a matter of the utmost importance to Beijing. And, not surprisingly, the Japanese are similarly preoccupied with China and its relationship with the United States. Particularly striking was the observation by Democratic Party of Japan President Yukio Hatoyama that, "We should make more efforts to reinforce China's confidence in Japan because we are not certain what the future holds for U.S.-China relations." Hatoyama added: "It cannot completely be ruled out that Washington and Beijing will not compete with each other over hegemony. Thus, it is potentially somewhat dangerous to consider it safe to always side with the United States." It is no exaggeration to say that whether Japan remains primarily allied with America, or instead arms itself and acts largely on its own in Asia, will be predominantly determined by how well or badly the United States handles its relations with China.[15]

The consequences of this triangular reality cut two ways. For China, the key implication is that Beijing would be wise to exercise self-restraint in its anti-American "hegemony" campaign. It could backfire badly for China. Overheated Chinese rhetoric about an anti-American coalition with Russia (and perhaps also with India) might prompt even stronger pressures in America on behalf of an anti-Chinese, U.S.-led alliance embracing not only Japan and South Korea but even Taiwan. Some in America might also advocate a strategic counter toward India, on the grounds that India is wary of China and that it shares America's democratic credentials. The Chinese should also be aware that latent but ingrown anti-Chinese sentiments, once given the opportunity, could quickly come to dominate Japanese politics.

In fact, anti-Chinese sentiments in Japan, especially in its foreign policy establishment, are visibly on the rise. In the words of Nobuo Miyamato, the Director of the Nomura Research Council,

> even though a joint declaration by Japan and China talks about a 'friendly and cooperative partnership', Japan and China will not be

able to extricate themselves from a relationship of political and strategic competition for the next 50-100 years.[16]

Open Sino-American hostility would most likely spur an intense arms race between Japan and China, to the detriment of both the stability of, and the American position in, the Far East. Though neither America nor Japan can exclude the possibility that China may, indeed, become a threat—and hence their alliance is also a form of insurance—it is neither in America's nor in Japan's interest to precipitate that threat. Hence an anti-Chinese alliance with a rearmed Japan should be America's last, and not first, strategic option.

Accordingly, for America the key implication is that the United States has to be very deliberate in balancing the inevitable readjustment in U.S.-Japan defense cooperation, pointing toward an enhanced international security role for Japan, with the imperative of sensitivity for Chinese concerns. The Chinese are convinced that Japan is irrevocably committed to significant remilitarization and that its sharp edge is pointed at China. The Chinese press very deliberately plays up any Japanese statements that can be construed as anti-Chinese. Thus even the most authoritative Chinese newspaper went into paroxysms of anger when the newly elected governor of Tokyo, Ishihara Shintaro—known also for his attacks on the United States—referred to Taiwan as Japan's "peripheral state."[17] The United States, therefore, must be especially careful to make certain that a more militarily powerful Japan is fully integrated into a larger cooperative security system in Northeast Asia and is not poised primarily as America's anti-Chinese ally.

It follows also that increasing U.S.-Japan security cooperation in the Far East should be designed in a manner that does not mimic NATO's originally overt focus on the Soviet Union's aggressive intentions. For the present, China does not have the capacity for genuinely serious regional aggression. Accordingly, ongoing U.S.-Japan-South Korea defense planning as well as joint exercises should avoid an overtly anti-Chinese cast. In addition, China should be included, as much as possible, in the emerging multilateral dialogue regarding regional security. It has taken years, and much American effort, to precipitate serious three-way U.S.-Japan-South Korea military discussions. Some four-way U.S.-Japan-China-South Korea defense consultations have also been initiated, and these may become gradually more formal. The key point to bear in mind here is that regional security in Northeast Asia is not a zero-sum game; how China is treated might well become a self-fulfilling prophesy.

The politically sensitive issue of Theater Missile Defense (TMD) is very germane to the above comments. Handled well, a TMD system could be regionally stabilizing; handled badly, it could spark intense U.S.-China hostility while setting off in Japan a polarizing and destabilizing debate over Japan's relations with the United States and with China. Accordingly, two important precautions are in order. The first is that no regional U.S.-Japan-South Korea TMD should include Taiwan either formally or through direct deployment. Taiwan can be de facto covered by a TMD located on U.S. naval platforms, thereby avoiding the Chinese charge that the United States is reverting by the back door to a formal defense arrangement with Taiwan. Secondly, consultations with the Chinese regarding any eventual missile system should be held on the same basis as proposed to Russia. There is no compelling reason to treat China differently.

More generally, it is also important to make the utmost effort to stimulate a comprehensive strategic dialogue with China regarding not only the security of Northeast Asia but of Eurasia more generally. Whenever possible, it should be a triangular dialogue, involving also the Japanese. Appropriate subjects should include the future of Russia (a topic rarely discussed in depth with the Chinese—yet of vital importance to China, given its far larger population, rapidly growing economy, and the emptiness of the neighboring Russian Far East[18]), the status of the Central Asian states (with their energy resources being of great interest to both China and Japan), stability in Southeast Asia, and the unstable relationship between nuclear-armed India and Pakistan. Developing and institutionalizing such a dialogue, and especially making it truly trilateral, will require a major effort and much time, but promoting it should be viewed as a high U.S. strategic priority.

Ten Basic Principles and Premises for U.S.–China Relations

1. The future orientation of China, and not the future of Taiwan, should be America's central strategic concern.

2. An anti-Chinese defense arrangement with Taiwan should not be indirectly revived, and U.S. arms sales should be carefully calibrated in relation to the state of U.S.-China relations and PRC capabilities.

3. Peaceful reunification can be promoted only by a democratizing and increasingly prosperous PRC on the basis of a "one country, several systems" formula.

4. Respect for human rights in China should be fostered by a policy of indirection focused on the benefits of the rule of law.

5. The U.S.-China-Japan relationship is highly interactive, in a manner reminiscent of the U.S.-European-Soviet relationship.

6. The United States should promote a trilateral strategic dialogue with China and Japan regarding the security of Eurasia.

7. A pre-emptive anti-Chinese defense coalition, based on TMD, could become a self-fulfilling prophecy of a hostile China.

8. The OSCE should be expanded to include Asia, following five-way security talks involving the United States, Europe, Russia, China and Japan.

9. The G-8 should be enlarged to G-9 by the inclusion of the PRC.

10. The ultimate U.S. goal should be a China that evolves into a genuinely vested partner in an increasingly cooperative Eurasian system.

Over time, a successful three-way dialogue, as well as a cooperative (and not unilateral) approach to the TMD issue, may foster a greater Chinese inclination to resolve peacefully the division of Korea. That division, the last major unresolved territorial-political legacy of the Cold War, is increasingly anomalous. However, its constructive resolution requires not only China's assent but its actual participation. That participation will become more likely when China begins to view itself as part of a larger security scheme in the Far East in which America and Japan are not perceived as its potential adversaries.

A three-way strategic dialogue could in turn pave the way for a broader Eurasian security forum, spanning America, Europe, Russia, China and Japan. The west of the Eurasian continent is already highly organized through NATO and the EU, and these integrated structures overlap with Eurasia's volatile "middle zone" through the fifty-four member Organization for Security and Cooperation in Europe (OSCE), which includes Russia and the Central Asian states. In the east, institutionalized security cooperation involves only the formal U.S.-Japan and U.S.-South Korea treaties as well as the informal Japan-South Korea consultations. China is not formally engaged, and there is no equivalent to the loosely cooperative OSCE. At the very least, a serious five-way strategic dialogue might prompt the redefinition of the letter *e* in OSCE from "European" to "Eurasian" through the inclusion in an expanded and redefined OSCE of a dozen or so Asian states.

Dealing China In

The task of assimilating China into a wider Eurasian equilibrium has to be pursued on other fronts as well. In addition to shaping a more sustained triangular relationship with China and Japan, China's accession to the WTO and the regularization of normal trade relations between the United States and China would be significant steps in the gradual integration of China into the world economy.

Much the same applies to the question of China's inclusion in the G-8 (which I have been advocating for more than three years).

The G-8 summit has become a hybrid, neither a forum for the democracies nor a conclave of the most advanced economies. That dual formula was compromised by the politically expedient decision to include Russia, hardly an advanced economy and questionably a democracy. Similar political expediency, therefore, should dictate the inclusion of the economically much more dynamic China, with the G-9 thereby becoming a more genuine global power forum. That would propitiate China's quest for status while also enhancing its stake in the emerging global system.

In some respects, China's international behavior is already no worse, and may be even better, than India's. New Delhi over the years backed various forms of Soviet aggression, went to war with its neighbors more often than China, flaunted its disregard for nuclear non-proliferation, used force to resolve some colonial legacies such as Goa, has been careless of human rights in Kashmir, and has proved no less obstreperous than China in the WTO negotiations. Yet no leading presidential candidate in America has labeled India as America's major "competitor," as was the case with China in late 1999. Obviously, India's democratic credentials give its external ambitions a more benign cast, but the comparison with India—like China a very poor, developing, but also politically aspiring power—should help to place in perspective the somewhat over-heated fears of China.

Still, it is important to reiterate that China is unlikely to become America's strategic partner again in the manner that it was during the decade starting with the late 1970s. The most that can reasonably be expected, barring a serious domestic or international crisis, is that China will gradually become an increasingly cooperative player in the international "game," in which the major participants play according to shared rules even while each keeps his own score. As a major regional player, China will occasionally collide with the United States, but it is also likely to find that its long-run interests are better served by observing common standards. China may thus become neither a formal ally nor a declared enemy of America but an important participant in the evolving international system, increasingly meeting and grudgingly accepting more and more of that system's conventions.

Such an internationally more cooperative China will have an important geostrategic effect on Eurasia. Given Russia's evident fears of China's larger economy and population, such a China will be much more likely to push Moscow toward the Atlanticist Europe than a China that is antagonistic toward the United States. At the same time, such a China will reinforce Japan's stake in a stable alliance with America without frightening Tokyo either into rapid rearmament or into divisive tensions with the United States.

It follows that the central strategic task of U.S. policy toward China should be nothing less than the attainment of a fundamental, truly historic shift in the mindset of the Chinese elite: to view China no longer as the self-isolated Middle Kingdom, or as the Celestial Empire, or as the aggrieved victim, or as the world's revolutionary center—but, more prosaically, as a vested partner in Eurasian stability and as a key player in the global system.

Notes

1. Kenneth Lieberthal, "A New China Strategy," *Foreign Affairs* (November/December 1995). Lieberthal has been a member of the Clinton NSC staff.

2. See the conclusion drawn by Z. M. Khalilzad et al., "The United States and China: Strategic and Military Implications" (Santa Monica, Calif.: RAND, 1999), p. 59

3. The full story of the productive U.S.-China cooperation directed against the Soviet Union (especially in regard to Afghanistan), initiated by the Carter administration and continued under Reagan, still remains to be told.

4. It has, of course, become a significant economic partner—the United States' fourth-largest trading partner, in fact. China's bilateral trade with the United States amounted to exports of $62.6 billion and imports of $12.9 billion in 1997. That same year, U.S. foreign direct investment in China was just over $5 billion.

5. Some top Chinese leaders have even speculated about the possibility of a U.S.-China military collision. In an address to senior PLA cadres, Zhang Wannian, the vice chairman of the Central Military Commission, bluntly stated in early 1999 that, "The possibility that a limited war may break out

between China and the United States does exist." *Cheng Ming* (Hong Kong monthly), April 1, 1999.

6. Shi Yinhong, "Scholar on Hegemonistic Interference," *Ta Kung Pao*, July 2, 1999, trans. by Foreign Broadcast Information Service (FBIS). More specifically, he warned that "the hegemonists could possibly intervene in China's affairs on the following issues: the Taiwan issue, the Tibet and Xinjiang issue, the South China Sea islands issue, China's internal political system or China's strategic weapons."

7. Ding Sheng, "The New Clinton Doctrine," *Xiandai Guoji Guanxi*, August 20, 1999, trans. by FBIS. An authoritative discussion of the alleged American plans to dominate Eurasia strategically, and to exploit to that end its various ethnic problems, is contained in an analysis of U.S.-Russia relations by Lu Zhongwei, "International Security Environment Goes Through Changes," *Beijing Review*, August 23, 1999.

8. "On Cultural Roots of the Sino-U.S. Conflict," *Ta Kung Pao*, September 21, 1999, trans. by FBIS.

9. An unusually candid presidential account of how normalization was effected is provided in Jimmy Carter, "The Real China Story," *Foreign Affairs* (November/December 1999).

10. It is estimated that up to 200,000 Taiwanese businessmen now work in the PRC, with Taiwanese investments in mainland China now well in excess of $20 billion, and another $25 billion planned. The PRC is now Taiwan's third-largest trade partner, following the United States and Japan.

11. Lee Teng-hui, "Understanding Taiwan," *Foreign Affairs* (November/December 1999).

12. The notion of a "sovereign" Taiwan was explicitly postulated in a public statement issued by a group of conservative foreign policy experts, some of whom play an active role in the ongoing presidential campaign. (Heritage Foundation press release, August 24, 1999.)

13. William S. Cohen, "The Security Situation in the Taiwan Strait," Report to the Congress pursuant to the FY99 Appropriations Bill (Washington, D.C.: Department of Defense, 1999).

14. The House passed a modified version of the act in February.

15. For a revealing discussion of Japan's relationship with China and the United States conducted by leading Japanese officials, see "Seeking True Independence, et al." (in Japanese), *Yomiuri Shimbun*, January 11, 2000.

16. *Chuo Koron* (February 1999), p. 247, trans. by FBIS.

17. See "Ishihara's Antics Worth High Vigilance," *Renmin Ribao*, November 17, 1999, trans. by FBIS.

18. Both the Russians and the Chinese are very sensitive to the demographic realities prevailing in Eurasia's eastern extremities. The population of Manchuria alone is 102.3 million and the density per square kilometer is 168. The total population of the four adjacent Russian regions is 6.1 million, with a population density of only 5.3 per square kilometer.

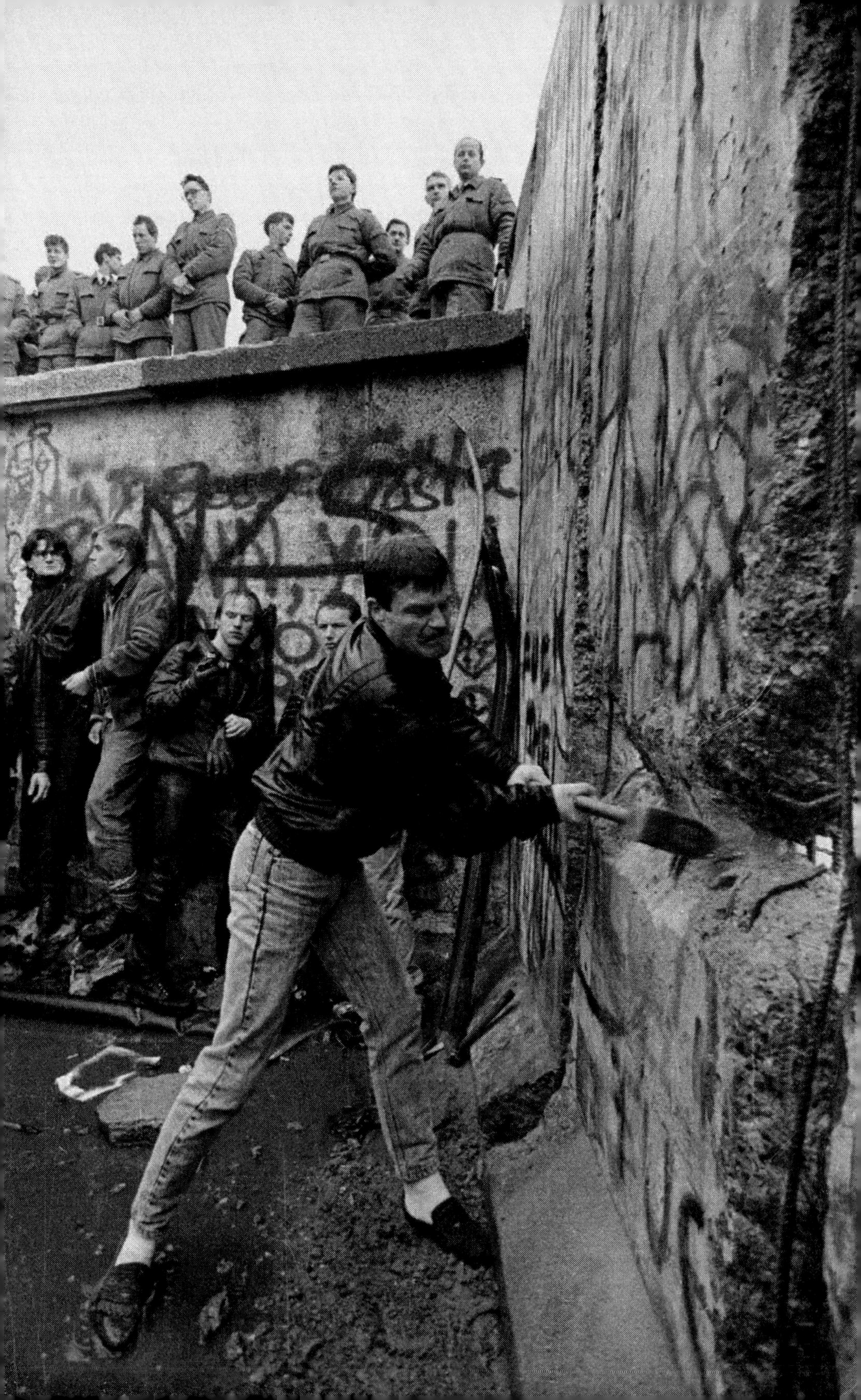

CHAPTER TWO

LIVING WITH A NEW EUROPE

THE TRANSATLANTIC ALLIANCE IS AMERICA'S MOST IMPORTANT GLOBAL relationship. It is the springboard for U.S. global involvement, enabling America to play the decisive role of arbiter in Eurasia—the world's central arena of power—and it creates a coalition that is globally dominant in all the key dimensions of power and influence. America and Europe together serve as the axis of global stability, the locomotive of the world's economy, and the nexus of global intellectual capital as well as technological innovation. Just as important, they are both home to the world's most successful democracies. How the U.S.-European relationship is managed, therefore, must be Washington's highest priority.

In the longer run, the appearance of a truly politically united Europe would entail a basic shift in the distribution of global power, with consequences as far-reaching as those generated by the collapse of the Soviet empire and by the subsequent emergence of America's global preponderance. The impact of such a Europe on America's own position in the world and on the Eurasian power balance would be enormous (see the table on the following page for an indication of how a united Europe would dwarf the United States), inevitably generating severe two-way transatlantic tensions. Presently, neither side is well equipped to handle such potentially significant change.

Reprinted with permission. "Living with a New Europe," *The National Interest* (Summer 2000).

Table 1. Comparing the United States with a United Europe

	United States	EU 15	EU 27*	EU 27 + Turkey
Population	272,639,608	374,324,512	479,779,201	545,378,407
GDP (purchasing power parity (in $ trillions)	$8.511	$8.053	$8.747	$9.172
GDP per capita	$31,500	$20,927	$15,061	$14,759
Military expenditures (in $ billions)	$267.2	$166.3	$221.6	$228.4
Military expenditures as % of GDP	3.4%	1.84%	1.97%	2.06%
Total exports (in $ trillions)	$0.905	$2.032	$2.189	$2.233
Exports as % of world total	16.5%	37.0%	39.9%	40.7%
Total imports (in $ trillions)	$0.757	$2.028	$2.146	$2.174
Imports as % of world total	13.5%	36.0%	38.1%	38.9%

Sources: *The World Factbook, 1999* (Washington, D.C.: Central Intelligence Agency, 1999). Export and import estimates are calculated from 1998 trade figures in *Direction of Trade Statistics Quarterly* (Washington, D.C.: International Monetary Fund, December 1999), 2–5.
* EU 27 consists of current members and all the potential candidates for membership in Central and Eastern Europe.

Americans generally do not fully comprehend the European desire for an upgraded status in the relationship and they lack a clear appreciation of the diversity of European views concerning the United States. Europeans often fail to grasp both the spontaneity and the sincerity of America's commitment to Europe, infusing into their perception of America's desire to sustain the Euro-Atlantic alliance a European penchant for Machiavellian duplicity.

It should be noted, however, that the operative words in the preceding paragraph regarding the significance of a truly united Europe are "would be." A European Union with genuine political weight and unity is not foreordained. The emergence of such a Europe depends on the depth of its political integration, on the scope of Europe's external expansion, and on the degree to which Europe develops its own military as well as political identity. The decisive steps in these regards have yet to be taken.

Currently, Europe—despite its economic strength, significant economic and financial integration, and the enduring authenticity of the transatlantic friendship—is a de facto military protectorate of the United States. This situation necessarily generates tensions and resentments, especially since the direct threat to Europe that made such dependence somewhat palatable has obviously waned. Nonetheless, it is not only a fact that the alliance between America and Europe is unequal, but it is also true that the existing asymmetry in power between the two is likely to widen even further in America's favor.

This asymmetry is due both to the unprecedented strength of America's economic expansion and to the technological innovation that America pioneers in such complex and diverse fields as biotechnology and information technology. What is more, the American-led technological revolution in military affairs enhances not only the scope of the military reach of the United States, but also transforms the very nature and uses of military power itself. Regardless of any collective action on the part of the European states, it is highly unlikely that Europe will be able to close the military gap with America at any point in the near future.

As a result, the United States is likely to remain the only truly global power for at least another generation. And that in turn means that America in all likelihood will also remain the dominant partner in the transatlantic alliance for the first quarter of the twenty-first century. It follows, therefore, that transatlantic debate will not be about fundamental alterations in the nature of the relationship, but rather about the implications of anticipated trends and the corresponding yet somewhat more marginal adjustments. That said, it hardly needs to be added that even incremental adaptations can breed conflicts, which should be avoided if the U.S.-European relationship is to remain constructive and truly cooperative.

HISTORICAL DIFFERENCES

A basic historical mystification both inspires and complicates the ongoing dialogue between America and Europe. Both sides instinctively think of America when they dream of a united Europe. The Europeans crave America's continental scale and global standing, and, in their more effervescent moments, they even envisage a future Europe as a global superpower co-equal to America. The Americans, when welcoming—occasionally somewhat skeptically—Europe's future unity, instinctively draw on their own historical experience. That vision renders some U.S. foreign policymakers uneasy, for the inescapable presumption is that Europe—when it "unites"—will become America's peer, and potentially its rival.

The American experience is often invoked by European statesmen in Europe's march to unity (one such figure recently declared to me that the European Union today is somewhere between 1776 and 1789). Yet most European political leaders realize that the European Union lacks both the ideological passion and the civic loyalty that inspired not only the framers of America's Constitution but—and this is the crucial test of political commitment—those prepared to make the ultimate sacrifice for the independence of the American colonies. As of now, and for the foreseeable future, it is simply the case that no "European" is willing to die for "Europe."

It follows that Europe, as it integrates, will be something altogether novel in the history of political entities, both in form and in substance. It will doubtless be a polity, in addition to being globally a most significant single economy. As a polity, however, it will lack the emotional and idealistic commitment that the United States evoked when it took shape. That commitment was expressed in a transcendental concept of political liberty, proclaimed to enjoy universal validity, that provided both the philosophical foundation and a politically attractive beacon for a new nation-state. The commitment of those who founded that state, and of those who later flocked to it and became assimilated by it, was almost religious. In short, the American revolution created a new kind of nationalism, one that was open to all, a nationalism with a universal face.

The Preamble to the U.S. Constitution conveys the singular character of that American commitment to national unity and liberty:

> We, the people of the United States, in order to form a more perfect Union, establish justice, insure domestic tranquillity, provide for the common defense, promote the general welfare, and secure the blessings of liberty to ourselves and our posterity, do ordain and establish . . .

Nothing quite like it characterizes the drumbeat of the European nations' march toward a common Europe. It is striking that the Treaty of Rome, the historic 1957 pledge of six European nations "to lay the foundations of an ever closer union," places emphasis in its very opening on ensuring "economic and social progress," on "constant improvements of the living and working conditions," on "the removal of existing obstacles" to "balanced trade and competition," on "the progressive abolition of restrictions on international trade," and so on. It is an admirably pragmatic, but also pedestrian, document.

To emphasize this essential difference between America and Europe is not to denigrate the historical significance of Europe's undertaking. Nor is it to question the good faith of those Europeans engaged in creating a new architecture. It is to note that the defining motivation of the European enterprise has, over time, become one of convenience and practicality. The initial impulse for European unity was more idealistic. Europe's "founding fathers" of the late 1940s and early 1950s were inspired by a transnational political conviction and very much motivated by the determination to end, once and for all, the nationalistic conflicts that twice in this century came close to destroying European civilization. They were also fearful that America, disenchanted by European feuds, might simply abandon the European nations to the other great historical option—also "unifying" in its own ugly way—the one east of the Cold War's new dividing line "from Stettin to Trieste."

Today's Europeans are serious about Europe in a more pragmatic way, though some—as noted earlier—do dream of an entity that will match America. French statesmen, at times unable to conceal their hyper-envy of America's global standing, see in Europe the recovery of France's past grandeur. The Germans have sought in Europe their own redemption. The British, more skeptical, have finally concluded that there will be a Europe of sorts and that they must be in it if they are to infuse some genuine significance into their own special relationship with America. Other peoples on the Continent—including the recently liberated peoples of Central Europe—also wish to be European, because they share the view that to be part of Europe is to be more secure, more prosperous and free. None of these motivations are base, all are historically justified, and they deserve America's respect.

Nonetheless, pragmatism differs in substance as well as in its effects from patriotism. A polity construed on convenience is bound to be different from a polity derived from conviction. The former can still generate loyalty. It can create a shared community. But it is also likely to be less ambitious, politically less assertive and, above all, less inclined toward idealism and personal sacrifice. Despite some similarities in scale, the "Europe" that is actually emerging is thus likely to be politically quite different from America: a hybrid of a huge transnational corporation, to which it is prudent and convenient and even gratifying to belong, and of a confederated state that over time may also gain the genuine loyalty of its hitherto distinctive communities. In short, the European polity of convenience will be less than a United States of Europe, though more than just a European Union Incorporated.

Indeed, it is no aspersion on anyone or any state to suggest that on the global scene the emerging Europe is likely to be more similar to a Switzerland writ large than to the United States. The Swiss constitution—which ended inter-communal strife—stresses that the ethnically differentiated Swiss Cantons resolved "to renew [their] alliance," that they were "determined to live [their] diversity in unity respecting one another," and went on to identify the practical purposes of the Confederation. Abroad, the main emphasis of Switzerland's international engagement has been in the important areas of international finance and trade, while avoiding engagement in this century's global political-philosophical conflicts.

Integration, Not Unification

In any case, it seems reasonable to conclude that "Europe," in the foreseeable future, will not be—indeed, cannot be—"America." Once the implications of that reality are digested on both sides of the Atlantic, the U.S.-European dialogue should become more relaxed, even as the Europeans address the dilemmas connected with their simultaneous quest for integration, expansion and some militarization; and even as the Americans adjust to the inevitable emergence of a novel European polity.

Unification of several peoples normally occurs as a result of external necessity, shared ideological commitment, domination by the most powerful, or some combination thereof. In the initial phase of the European quest for unity all three factors were at play, though in varying degrees: the Soviet Union was a real threat; European idealism was nurtured by the still fresh memories of World War II; and France, exploiting West Germany's sense of moral vulnerability, was able to harness Germany's rising economic potential in support of its own political ambitions. By the end of the century, these impulses have perceptibly waned. As a result, European "integration"—largely a process of regulatory standardization—has become the alternative definition of unification. Yet while integration is a perfectly sensible way of achieving an operationally effective merger, a merger still falls quite short of an emotionally meaningful marriage.

The plain fact is that bureaucratically spearheaded integration simply cannot generate the political will needed for genuine unity. It can neither stir the imagination (despite the occasional rhetoric about Europe becoming America's peer) nor develop the mortal passion that can sustain a nation-state in a time of adversity. The 80,000 page-long *acquis communautaire* (organized into 31 policy sectors)—which a new member of the European Union must ratify—is not likely to provide the average European with the needed nourishment for politically energizing loyalty. However, it should be reiterated that by now, given the absence of the other three more traditional ways of seeking unity, integration is not only necessary but is the *only* way that Europe can move forward toward "unity."

That gap between "unification" and "integration," in turn, explains why integration is bound to be slow; and why, were it somehow accelerated too sharply, it could even divide Europe once again. Indeed, any attempt to accelerate political unification would probably intensify internal tensions between the leading states within the Union, since each of them still insists on preserving its sovereignty in the critical area of foreign policymaking. At this stage, anti-Americanism as the impetus for unity—even when disguised by talk of "multipolarity"—cannot be a unifying force as anti-Sovietism once was, because most Europeans do not subscribe to it. Moreover, with Germany reunited, no one in Europe, outside of Paris, still regards France as the putative leader of the new Europe—but also no one in Europe desires Germany to become Europe's dominant leader.

Integration, however, is not only a slow process, but each successful step increases the very complexity of the undertaking. Integration inherently means an incremental and highly balanced progression toward deepening interdependence among constituent units, but their growing interdependence is not infused with the unifying political passion required for the assertion of genuine global independence. That may happen eventually, when Europeans come to view themselves politically as Europeans while remaining, for example, German or French as a matter of linguistic and cultural peculiarity.

Horizontal Expansion

In the meantime, because of Europe's slow progression, external expansion is likely to become a partial compensation for the crawling pace of internal integration. Europe will grow, but more horizontally than vertically since, as a practical matter, the two cannot significantly advance at the same time. This painful reality is a sensitive point among Europe's true believers. When Jacques Delors dared to declare flatly in early 2000 that "the pace [of enlargement] is unquestionably being forced . . . we thus risk diluting the blueprint" for European integration, with the result that "we will inevitably move away from a political Europe as defined by Europe's founding fathers," he was almost immediately and publicly taken to task by a compatriot EU Commissioner, Michel Barnier.

The Commissioners in Brussels hope that bureaucratic streamlining and institutional renewal will invigorate the process of integration. Buoyed by the modest success of the euro—despite some apocalyptic predictions from its largely American and British detractors—Brussels has moved forward, in anticipation of significant expansion, with the long-standing inter-governmental conference on the renewal of the European institutions. Key institutional decisions are to be made by the end of the year. But even the most forceful proponents of expansion concede that, at best, politically significant integration will have to be confined for a while to the smaller inner core of the EU, thus perhaps creating a so-called "multi-speed and variable geometry" Europe.[1] Yet even if that were to happen, it is doubtful that this formula would resolve the basic tension between integration and expansion in so far as the development of a common foreign policy is concerned. Such a Europe would mean division into first and second-class members, with the latter objecting to any major foreign policy decisions taken on their behalf by a directorate of allegedly more truly European states.

In any case, enlargement, too, is bound to become an increasingly absorbing and complicated task. With some two hundred EU teams about to begin the tedious process of negotiating the modalities of accession with the dozen or so new aspirant nations, expansion will probably slow down, both because of its inherent complexity and because of a lack of will on the part of EU member states. In fact, the admission of any Central European state by 2004 is becoming increasingly problematic. In the longer run, however, expansion cannot be avoided. An amputated Europe cannot be a true Europe. A geopolitical void between Europe and Russia would be dangerous. Moreover, an aging Western Europe would begin to stagnate economically and socially.[2] No wonder, then, that some leading European planners have begun to advocate a Europe of as many as thirty-five to forty members by the year 2020—a Europe that would be geographically and culturally whole, but almost certainly politically diluted.[3]

A Decalogue Regarding European Developments and Prospects

1. For most Europeans, "Europe" is not an object of personal affection. It is more a convenience than a conviction.

2. On the global scene, the EU will not be like America but more like a Switzerland writ large.

3. Most Europeans do not partake of anti-Americanism as the impulse for unity.

4. Integration is essentially a bureaucratic process and not the same as unification.

5. The EU's expansion inevitably collides with deepening integration.

6. The EU needs to expand for demographic and economic reasons.

7. A federated inner core of foreign-policymaking states within a larger EU of 21 or more states is not politically workable.

8. Slow expansion plus bureaucratic integration is likely to produce a Europe united economically but only confederated politically.

9. The EU is unlikely to acquire an autonomous military capability.

10. The EU will thus be a novel type of polity, with its global influence primarily economic and financial.

A Question of Muscle

Thus, neither integration nor expansion is likely to create the truly European Europe that some Europeans crave and some Americans fear. Indeed, an increasing number of Europeans do sense that the combination of the euro and integration with slow expansion can only create economic sovereignty. Political awareness that more is needed prompted the three leading European states—France, Great Britain and Germany—to join in 1999 in an effort to create a credible European military capability, and to do so even before an integrated Europe with a defining foreign policy of its own emerges. The projected European military force is meant to put some muscle behind a common foreign and security policy (CFSP), which is to be shaped by the newly created post of Europe's High Representative for External Relations and Common Security.

The proposed joint European rapid reaction force, which is to be operational by 2003, will be the first tangible manifestation of a political Europe. In contrast to the already existing, but largely symbolic, "Eurocorps"—composed primarily of French, German, Spanish and other draftees and possessing neither mobility nor real military capability—the planned force would be assembled when needed from pre-dedicated combat units, would number up to 60,000 men deployable within 60 days, and would be sustainable in a theater of deployment "in or around Europe" for at least a year. In effect, according to various European estimates, such a force would be equivalent to a full corps, supported by some 150 to 300 aircraft, 15 large combat vessels, a strategic air transport capability, and the requisite C3I (command, control, communications and intelligence). European military experts are to conduct an accelerated audit of the inventory of the available European assets so that the force can engage in peacekeeping or even in some (otherwise unspecified) limited combat operations. Its appearance would mark the emergence of a genuine European Security and Defense Identity (ESDI), capable of military action outside of NATO.

However, the European defense initiative—driven by the genuinely felt sense of Europe's military inadequacy revealed by the Kosovo war, fueled by French ambitions, but tempered by British and

German inclinations to reassure the Americans—has yet to pass three basic tests: will the force be rapidly deployable, will it be militarily capable, and will it be logistically sustainable? Europe has the means to create such a force; the question is whether it has the will.

At this stage, skepticism is very much in order. European defense leaders have stated that the force can be assembled without additional expenditures through a very deliberate reallocation of existing defense budget items, a proposition that defies common sense. It is evident to serious European commentators that the planned force will require improvements in central logistics control, joint military depots, and presumably some joint exercises. That would entail additional costs, not to mention the more basic need for adequate reconnaissance and intelligence as well as for a more competitive and more consolidated European defense industry. Yet in recent years the overall percentage of the European budgets allocated to defense as well as to defense-related R&D has actually been declining, with European defense expenditures having fallen in real terms by about 22 percent since 1992.

The critical fact is that political parsimony undermines the military seriousness of the venture. As Daniel Vernet wrote in *Le Monde* in September 1999, for the European force to come into being, the Europeans "must know exactly what they want, define defense restructuring programs (politically sensitive and financially costly), and, finally, allocate the budgetary resources to match their ambitions." In addition, to sustain a force of 60,000 men in the field for more than a year, a rotational pool of about 180,000 combat-ready European soldiers must be available. It is not.

A further complication, casting additional doubt on the credibility of the proposed enterprise, is that some European states are members of the EU but not of NATO (the "neutrals"), and others of NATO but not of the EU (America's "Trojan horses," according to some Europeanists). Their prospective relationship to ESDI is thus unclear and, in any case, it inevitably complicates the picture. Finally, but perhaps most important of all, the meshing of the proposed force with existing NATO arrangements could become disruptive operationally and divisive politically.

Ultimately, the most probable outcome for ESDI is that the proposed force will produce neither a rival to NATO nor the long-missing second European "pillar" for a more equal alliance. Although the Europeans will probably somewhat enhance their own military planning and joint command structures, especially after the expected absorption of the Western European Union by the EU itself, more likely is the piecemeal emergence over the next five or so years of a somewhat improved European capability to provide for non-NATO peacekeeping in some not overly violent European trouble spot (most likely in the Balkans). In effect, the so-called European pillar will be made less out of steel and concrete and more out of *papier-mâché*. As a result, Europe will fall short of becoming a comprehensive global power. Painful as it may be for those who would like to see a politically vital Europe, most Europeans still remain unwilling not only to die but even to pay for Europe's security.

FOR STRATEGIC DIRECTION

U.S. policymakers should keep in mind a simple injunction when shaping American policy toward Europe: do not make the ideal the enemy of the good. The ideal from Washington's point of view would be a politically united Europe that is a dedicated member of NATO—one spending as much on defense as the United States but committing the funds almost entirely to the upgrading of NATO's capabilities; willing to have NATO act "out of area" in order to reduce America's global burdens; and remaining compliant to American geopolitical preferences regarding adjacent regions, especially Russia and the Middle East, and accommodating on such matters as international trade and finance. The good is a Europe that is more of a rival economically, that steadily enlarges the scope of European interdependence while lagging in real political-military independence, that recognizes its self-interest in keeping America deployed on the European periphery of Eurasia, even while it chafes at its relative dependence and half-heartedly seeks gradual emancipation.

U.S. policymakers should recognize that "the good" actually serves vital American interests. They should consider that initiatives such as

ESDI reflect the European quest for self-respect, and that carping injunctions—a series of "do nots" emanating both from the State and Defense Departments—merely intensify European resentments and have the potential to drive the Germans and the British into the arms of the French. Moreover, American opposition to the effort can only serve to convince some Europeans—wrongly—that NATO is more important to U.S. security than it is to Europe's. Last but not least, given the realities of the European scene, what ESDI poses for NATO are problems of process not ones of principle, and problems of process are not likely to be constructively managed by elevating them into issues of principle.

Hence, dramatic warnings of "decoupling" are counterproductive. They have a theological ring to them, and as such they threaten to transform differences that can be accommodated into ones involving doctrinal debates. They are reminiscent of earlier NATO collisions that accomplished nothing good—whether over the abortive Multilateral Nuclear Force initiative of the early 1960s, which accelerated the French nuclear program; or, more recently, the brief spasm in 1999 of American-pushed efforts to revamp NATO into some sort of a global ("out of area") alliance, which quickly came down to earth with the outbreak of the Kosovo war. Such disputes detract and distract from a fundamental reality: NATO, a truly remarkable success, may be far from perfect but it does not require a dramatic overhaul.

One should pause here and ask: Even assuming that the new European force were to come into being by 2003, where and how could it act on its own? What credible scenario can one envisage in which it could act decisively, without advance guarantees of NATO support and without some actual dependence on NATO assets? Let us assume a conflict in Estonia, with the Kremlin stirring up the Russian minority and then threatening to intervene; Europe would not lift a finger without direct NATO involvement. Suppose Montenegro secedes and Serbia invades; without U.S. participation, the planned European force would probably be defeated. While social unrest in some European province—say, Transylvania, or even Corsica!—might prove more susceptible to a deployment of European peacekeepers (much as has been the case in Bosnia), such an intervention is hardly an example of Europe becoming "an independent actor on the international stage," to quote French Defense Minister Alain Richard.

In a genuinely serious mission, the planned European force still would have to rely heavily on NATO assets in the key areas of reconnaissance, intelligence and airlift. These assets are primarily American, though dedicated to NATO. Thus, NATO would be de facto involved, even if initially it had exercised its option of first refusal. In brief, if the crisis is serious, the European reaction will not be independent; if the reaction is independent, the crisis will not be serious.

To be sure, adjustments within NATO will be unavoidable as Europe slowly evolves into a more defined polity. ESDI will make NATO's decision-making processes somewhat more cumbersome, and European contributions to NATO's own military enhancement may even marginally suffer as the EU seeks some sort of force of its own. ESDI, especially after the Europeans organize within the EU some sort of a European defense organism, will also have the effect of stimulating a shared European strategic perspective, which America will have to take into account. But a shared European security posture is more likely to emerge through the gradual consolidation of the European defense industry[4] and intensified European military planning than through any precipitous leap—especially by 2003—into an autonomous European combat capability.

Indeed, of greater consequence to NATO's future than the European under-performance revealed during the Kosovo war is Europe's nonperformance *after* the Kosovo war. The staggering fact is that "Europe" not only cannot protect itself but cannot even police itself. The inability of the European states to engage entirely on their own in effective peacekeeping in a small and weak region—and their reluctance to provide the needed financing for its economic recovery—poses a more serious long-term challenge to NATO's cohesion than does ESDI. It is likely to breed growing American uneasiness regarding the proper role for U.S. forces committed to Europe's defense.

In the nearer term, an even more divisive issue—one of greater strategic import—may be generated by U.S. plans to deploy a missile defense system. The ongoing debate in the United States over missile defense has been driven primarily by domestic political considerations, and a unilateral American decision, made in the heat of a U.S. presidential race, would doubtless be badly received in Europe. Indeed, American unilateralism on this matter could have far graver consequences than even the most intense U.S. concerns regarding ESDI's alleged "decoupling" effect on American and European security. If transatlantic security ties are to be sustained as America's central strategic priority, it is clearly better at this stage to engage in comprehensive discussions with America's allies regarding the feasibility, the costs, the defense trade-offs, and the political as well as strategic effects of a missile defense deployment. In any case, it is too early to make a prudent judgment as to how urgently needed and how practicable such a defensive shield may be. That is a decision for the next U.S. president to make.

In the meantime, a basic strategic priority of the United States should be the continued expansion of NATO. NATO enlargement offers the best possible guarantee of continued transatlantic security ties. It serves to create a more secure Europe, with fewer areas of geopolitical ambiguity, while increasing the European stake in a vital and credible alliance. Indeed, the case can be made that the 1999 NATO decision to return to the issue of enlargement no earlier than 2002 should be revised, and that a serious effort to decide on new members should be made in 2001, once a new U.S. president is in office. Several countries appear to be ready for inclusion, meeting not only the standards set recently for Poland, the Czech Republic and Hungary, but even previously for Spain. An earlier resumption of the process of enlargement would provide a clear signal that not only does the transatlantic security link remain vital, but that America and Europe are both serious about shaping a secure Europe that is truly European in scope.

American support for the resumption of NATO enlargement is consistent with the American stake in expansion of the EU. The larger Europe becomes, the less likely it is that either external or internal threats will pose a serious challenge to international peace. Moreover, in the longer run the more overlap there is in membership between NATO and the EU, the greater will be the cohesion of the transatlantic community and the more compelling the complementarity of the

A Decalogue of Basic U.S. Policy Premises and Guidelines

1. Europe remains America's natural and pre-eminent ally.

2. An Atlanticist Europe is essential to a stable Eurasian equilibrium.

3. An autonomous European defense capability, in any case unlikely in the near future, should not be opposed by the United States.

4. Allied political unity is more important than the enhancement of NATO's capabilities.

5. The United States should defer any deployment decision regarding a ballistic missile defense system until consensus is reached with NATO allies.

6. The United States should seek an enlarged NATO in Europe but not an "out of area" NATO.

7. The United States has a bigger stake in Europe's enlargement than in Europe's integration.

8. NATO and the EU should work together on joint plans for further expansion.

9. Eventually, Turkey, Cyprus and Israel might be included in both entities.

10. There should be no a priori limitations or exclusions on NATO and EU memberships.

Atlanticist and Europeanist visions. It is a felicitous fact that some of the candidates currently qualified for either NATO or EU membership happen to be the same countries. The United States can argue persuasively that Slovenia, Slovakia and Lithuania already meet, or are close to meeting, the criteria for NATO membership. According to a comparative study prepared by PricewaterhouseCoopers, several Central European states (including Slovenia and Estonia) are more qualified—in terms of macroeconomic stability, GNP, economic interaction with the EU, and economic infrastructure—for EU membership than was Greece. Poland and the Czech Republic—both already NATO members—were recently listed in the *Economist* as being more qualified than Italy! Which makes it all the more egregious that "the present accession requirements are more numerous and stringent than those that were faced by the South European countries that joined the EU earlier."[5]

That some countries merit entry into the EU and NATO should facilitate and encourage stronger U.S. support for the enlargement of both. High-level NATO-EU consultations regarding a staged, progressive and continuing expansion therefore would be very much in order. But it is premature at this stage even to speculate as to what might be the eventual outer boundaries of the two, hopefully overlapping, entities. Much will depend on the evolution of Russia, for whom the doors to an Atlanticist Europe should be kept open. An expanded EU overlapping with NATO can encourage Russia's positive evolution by dampening old imperial temptations. Russia may then recognize its own interest in accommodating and becoming associated with NATO. If it does not, then a larger NATO will provide the needed security for a larger Europe. But in any case, the a priori exclusion of any qualified European state from either NATO or the EU would be unwise.

Moreover, from a geopolitical as well as economic point of view, it is not too early to note that once both NATO and the EU have expanded to include the Baltic and some southeastern European states, the subsequent inclusion not only of Turkey but of Cyprus (following a Turkish-Greek accommodation) and of Israel (following a comprehensive peace with all its neighbors) may also become desirable. In addition, as Europe expands, the transatlantic community at some point will have to respond to signals from countries such as Ukraine, Georgia and even Azerbaijan, that their long-term objective is to qualify for participation in the great historical undertaking occurring within the EU and under NATO's security umbrella.

In promoting this great project, the United States should remain supportive of the EU's quest for deeper integration, even though that support will be mainly rhetorical. The United States has wisely avoided identifying itself with the conservative British opposition to Europe's political as well as monetary unity, and it should likewise avoid the occasional temptation to display *Schadenfreude* when Europe stumbles. Precisely because European integration will be slow and because the European polity will not be like America, America need not fear the emergence of a rival. The transatlantic relationship is more like a marriage that blends together mutually respected differences—including some division of labor—as well as commonalties, and both in fact serve to consolidate the partnership. That has been the case over the last half century, and it will remain so for some time to come.

In fact, the evolving character of the international system should reinforce the transatlantic bond. Europe and the United States account jointly for less than 15 percent of the world's population and are highly visible as islands of prosperity and privilege in a seething and restless global environment. In this age of instant communications, an awareness of inequality can be rapidly translated into political hostility targeted at those who are envied. Hence, both self-interest and a sense of potential vulnerability should continue to provide the underpinning for a durable U.S.-European alliance.

The European polity, situated on the western edge of Eurasia and in the immediate proximity of Africa, is more exposed to the risks inherent in rising global tumult than the politically more cohesive, militarily more powerful and geographically more isolated America. The Europeans will be more immediately at risk if a chauvinistic imperialism should again motivate Russian foreign policy, or if Africa and/or south-central Asia suffer worsening social failures. The proliferation of nuclear or other weapons of mass destruction also will endanger Europe more, given Europe's limited military capabilities and the proximity of potentially threatening states. For as far as one can see, Europe will continue to need America to be truly secure.

At the same time, a close relationship with Europe philosophically legitimates and gives focus to America's global role. It creates a community of democratic states without which the United States would be lonely in the world. Preserving, enhancing and especially enlarging that community—in order to "secure the blessings of liberty to ourselves and our posterity"—must therefore remain America's historically vital task.

Notes

1. "Variable geometry implies that the willing and able will be permitted to deepen the level of their integration in specific policy areas, while the unwilling will not be obliged to follow suit. A multi-speed approach implies that, while the willing and able proceed with integration in a given policy area, the willing but unable will have a clear road-map of how they can join at a later date." Robin Niblett, "The European Disunion," *The Washington Quarterly* (Winter 1997), pp. 104-5.

2. The OECD estimates that the EU will need 35 million immigrants in the next 25 years to keep the population at 1995 levels, and an additional 150 million by 2025 if it wishes to keep the current ratio of retirees to workers. Moreover, it is estimated that by 2030, state pensions will absorb 5.5 percent of the GDP in Britain, 13.5 in France, 16.5 in Germany and 20.3 in Italy. (The equivalent estimate for the United States is 6.6.)

3. According to a report prepared by Jacques Attali at the request of the French foreign minister, France—"combining continental generosity and strategic coherence"—should deliberately "promote what it can no longer avoid," namely, a Europe that embraces 35 or even 40 members, including among others Ukraine and Georgia, thereby opting for "pluralism" over federalism. Contrarily, Werner Weidenfeld has warned recently in *Frankfurter Allgemeine Zeitung* that "this clear abandoning of any attempt to deepen the European identity will turn out to be Europe's Achilles' Heel."

4. A significant step in that direction was taken during 1999 through the merger of Aerospatiale Matra SA and DaimlerChrysler Aerospace AG to create the European Aeronautic, Defense and Space Co., with resources and capabilities that are competitive by American standards.

5. Eva Ehrlich and Gabor Revesz, *The State of the Economy in Central and Eastern Europe Compared with the EU's Requirements* (Budapest: The Hungarian Academy of Sciences, 1999), p. 4.

Annex: A Dialogue

Daniel Vernet, director for international relations, *Le Monde*

Zbigniew Brzezinski knows exactly where a European defense force could be deployed: in Corsica! Thank you, Doctor. We already have the French gendarmerie, a kind of national guard that is in great demand in Bosnia and Kosovo, for that.

More seriously, Brzezinski represents the benevolent side of the American attitude toward the European integration process, including the attempt to build European projection forces allegedly capable of acting independently of NATO. He does not criticize this decision. He does not recommend that Washington should undermine it. He does not transform it into a problem of principle, which could divide the two sides of the Atlantic. Being more than skeptical about the ability of the Europeans to accomplish what they have embarked upon, he gives the American administration a piece of sound advice: do not fear the emergence of a rival. Brzezinski has a good case, underpinned by arguments that are hardly dismissible. Let me stress a few of them:

1. Integration has replaced unification as the ultimate goal of the European process. It will be a slow process, as a too speedy one could divide Europe rather than unite it.

2. Europe will grow horizontally rather than vertically, and widening is not compatible with deepening.

3. ESDI—the European Security and Defense Identity—does not represent a threat to NATO because, even in the most optimistic hypothesis, it will be effective only in unserious crises.

4. NATO and the EU should extend at the same pace, excluding no country a priori and including close association with Russia. Russia should recognize that this combined NATO-EU enlargement does not contradict its own interests. If it does not do so, NATO and EU enlargements will be needed to provide security to an expanded Europe.

Brzezinski seems to accept the Attali vision of a Europe from the Atlantic to Vladivostok, which is inconsistent with the dream of the founding fathers of the Common Market and the European Community. That dream envisaged the new Europe not only as a free-trade zone but as an international actor, a political partner for America—maybe not a global power for this generation or the next one, but a regional power, not only overcoming the historical conflicts between its member states but exporting security and possibly prosperity to its "near abroad."

Brzezinski is right: there is a contradiction between this vision—traditionally supported by every French government but not necessarily shared by all its partners in the EU—and the present shape of Europe. He is also right to point out that this situation will probably not change in the next few years. In some matters (the institutions, for example) Europe is more likely to accommodate the existing framework than to make the profound changes needed by a *grand bond en avant*. In other matters (such as defense), it lacks either the will or the means, or both, to have a common policy; in particular, it lacks the political will to allocate more resources to defense budgets, without which it will be impossible for Europe to have a common foreign and security policy.

All these points are indisputable. However, the future of the European Union does not look quite as bleak as described by Brzezinski. Up to now, Europe has not reached a point of no return, which could make the original vision impossible. Furthermore, every measure taken in the last decade—single market, euro, free circulation of people inside Europe (the so-called "Schengenland"), nomination of a High Representative for External Relations and Common Security, a modest but realistic step toward a European defense—leaves open the possibility of future improvements, even if they would not be spectacular ones. All options are still on the table.

Take the projection forces. Brzezinski rightly notes that the European reaction will not be independent if the crisis is serious. For the time being, that is certainly so. But an independent reaction in a less than vital conflict would be a major step forward compared with the inability and unwillingness of the Europeans to act in some low-intensity crises of recent years. Let us take the first step before the second.

Europe will not be a military power, but it will not set limits to its ambition and be a soft power, the kind of larger Switzerland Brzezinski refers to.

Since the end of World War II the American attitude regarding European integration has always been ambiguous: unify, but not too much. The end of the Cold War has not altered this ambivalence: poor Europe that is incapable of going beyond a limited integration; happy America that has such an ally.

Christoph Bertram, contributing editor, *Foreign Policy*

For all its many good points, Brzezinski's prescription for the future U.S.-European relationship is, in the final analysis, a complacent and hence a flawed one. It can be summed up in one sentence: Europe, far from turning into a rival for the United States, will remain a dependent variable, a useful tool for U.S. strategy to spread stability to as many countries outside Russia as possible by incorporating them; it should be humored but not regarded as an equal partner by the United States.

On one issue Brzezinski is right: there is no need for Americans to panic as the EU tries to speed up defense integration. The angry fluster in some Washington corridors caused by plans for modest if urgent improvements in European capabilities for "out of area" military intervention has no justification: whatever comes of the plan, in the event European forces will have to draw on U.S. assets and hence to gain prior U.S. agreement.

But to make military power the litmus test of European integration is to repeat Stalin's mistake of judging the Catholic Church by the number of its divisions. Even Brzezinski, that most European of American realpolitikers, does not understand what this emerging Europe is really about. For him, it is "a polity construed on convenience," not "conviction," a pragmatic device for shared prosperity and stability. But pragmatism fails to explain the extent to which proud states, steeped in their respective histories, have sacrificed national autonomy for European interdependence. What drove them to submit to the authority of common laws and a common supreme court, to create a common currency, to unite the western part of the Continent, to invite the new democracies of the rest of Europe into their midst, and now to try and develop the means for autonomous military action was never merely convenience. It was, and is, a certain idea of what Europe should be.

The power of this idea should not be underrated. Americans used to recognize this, patiently but persistently encouraging efforts at European integration during all the decades of the Cold War. Now, perhaps out of irritation over Europe's new-found confidence, coupled with a one-track fascination with their own military and technological prowess and the dizziness of grandeur that has descended upon the world's only and probably last superpower, Americans seem to have lost both the patience and the vision. Sadly, Brzezinski here provides a strategic rationale for this loss.

It is shortsighted nevertheless, and for the very reasons the author himself states so eloquently at the beginning of his article: "America and Europe together serve as the axis of global stability." There is no other similar partner for an America that cares about international order, prosperity and democratic progress. And Europe, whatever its shortcomings, is a much stronger partner today than during the Cold War. It will be stronger still in the future.

Therefore it should be America's prime interest to lay the foundations today for a partnership with the Europe of tomorrow. U.S. supremacy may last for a generation but it will not last forever. What better use to make of this temporary advantage than to establish now the institutional framework for a partnership in which a Europe that will be stronger than it is today and an America that will be weaker can work together for order, prosperity and democracy in tomorrow's world? That, Dr. Brzezinski, would be imaginative realpolitik!

Timothy Garton Ash, fellow of St. Antony's College, Oxford

As I would always expect from Zbigniew Brzezinski, this essay is lucid, incisive, far-reaching and stimulating. I have the problem of agreeing with most of its analysis and policy recommendations, especially those on NATO and EU enlargement. Let me nonetheless, as an English European, tease out five points, partly in disagreement, partly in necessary elaboration.

First, I am always in favor of saying things that are true, even if they are politically unhelpful. The statement that Europe is a "de facto military protectorate of the United States" seems to me neither true nor helpful. If I say "Xanadu is a French protectorate," this is generally understood to mean that the French run Xanadu. The Americans do not run Europe. Even in the weaker sense of "being dependent for military protection" this statement is scarcely true since, chaotic though Europe's defense arrangements are, there are no major current threats to our security against which the major European powers could not defend themselves and their EU partners.

Second, it is, however, true that even the strongest EU countries are still pathetically reliant on the United States in the case of any actual military action beyond the frontiers of the EU, even in a small patch of our own backyard such as Kosovo. I think one could usefully spell out that one major reason for this is that the leaders of Western Europe set the wrong priorities at the end of the Cold War, putting the creation of a common currency before that of a common army. With the present initiatives for improved foreign policy and defense coordination, the EU is doing in 2000 what it should have done in 1990. (I make the argument in more detail in my new book, *History of the Present*.)

Third, Brzezinski is absolutely right about the urgent need for the United States to be seen to be supporting, rather than carping at, these belated initiatives, especially in the defense field. The top-level political message from the new administration in Washington should be entirely and emphatically positive: "We *want* Europe to have a stronger defense identity and effective rapid reaction force." The supplementary stick might usefully be: "and we now expect you to look after Kosovo yourselves." Justified reservations about NATO compatibility can all be explored at lower, more technical levels.

Fourth, yes, Europe will never be a country. But (partly by means of introspection) I am not so pessimistic as Brzezinski is about the possibilities of positive emotional identification with Europe. Indeed, I think we have mutual friends in Central Europe who could well imagine "dying for Europe." *Malgré tout,* Europe has a soul. There is a struggle going on for this soul. Crudely stated, this is a new version of the old argument between the Atlanticist, liberal, global free-trading orientation, and the Gaullist, étatist, protectionist one. Historically, the balance of advantage has been moving from the latter to the former.

Fifth, by what it does and says, the United States will significantly affect this struggle, for better or for worse. Neither expecting a United States of Europe, nor accepting a Europe as Greater Switzer-land, it should work toward two goals best defined by one George Bush (Sr.): "partners in leadership" and "Europe whole and free."

Brzezinski replies:

Actually, in the main I agree with the basic points made by my friendly European critics. I do wish that America had Europe for a genuine partner, but wishful thinking is not a good guide to real policymaking. Creating a larger and gradually more integrated European space, closely allied to the United States, is the only game in town; the alternative to it is stagnation in the European venture, and a renewal of geopolitical uncertainties in the area between the Euro-Atlantic zone and Russia.

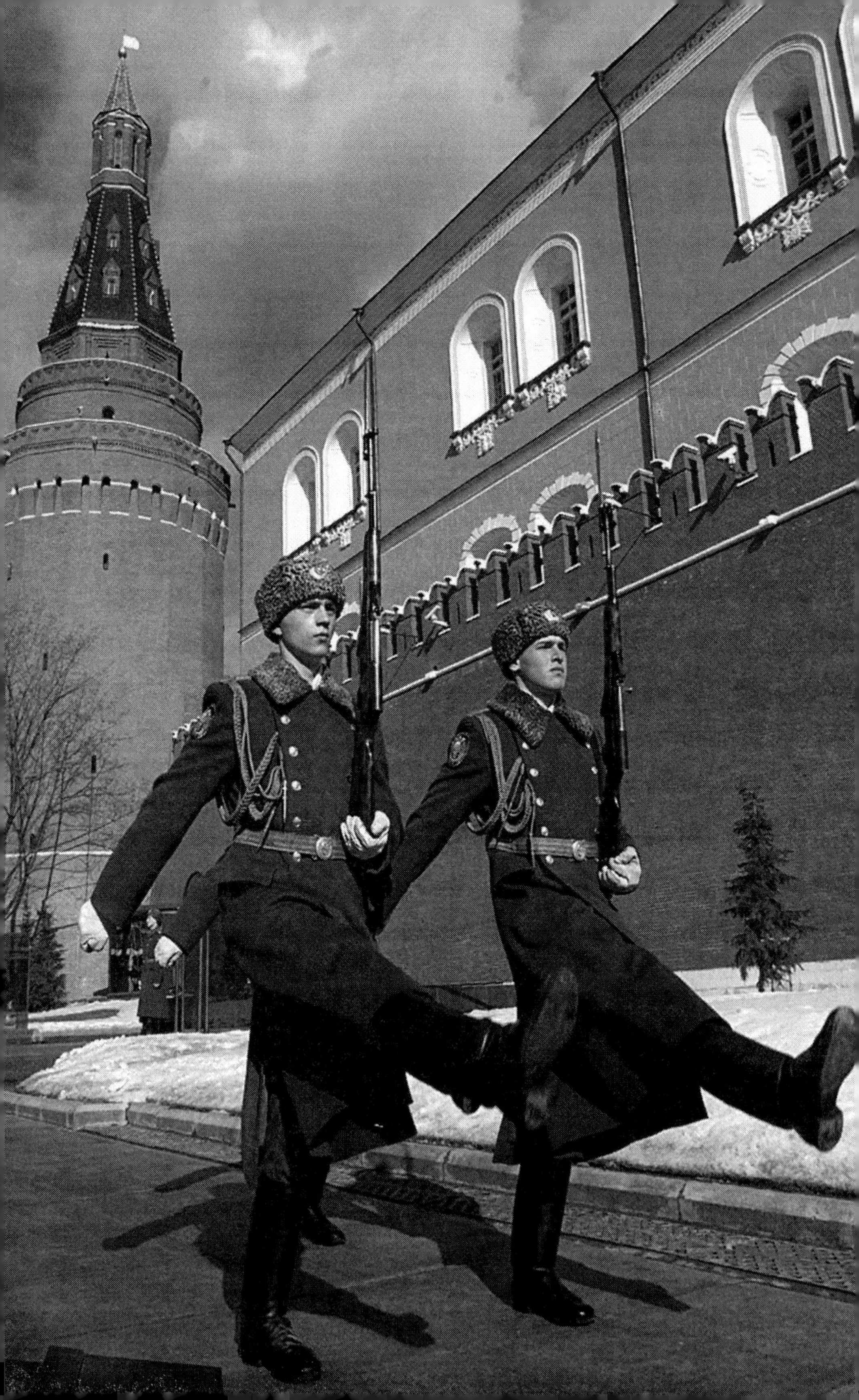

CHAPTER THREE

LIVING WITH RUSSIA

THE PROGRESSIVE INCLUSION OF RUSSIA IN THE EXPANDING TRANSATLANTIC community is the necessary component of any long-term U.S. strategy to consolidate stability on the Eurasian mega-continent. The pursuit of that goal will require patience and strategic persistence. There are no shortcuts on the way. Geostrategic conditions must be created that convince the Russians that it is in Russia's own best interest to become a truly democratic and European post-imperial nation-state—a state closely engaged to the transatlantic community.

Of the major Eurasian entities (the European Union, Russia, China, and Japan), only Europe and Japan can be said to recognize fully their fundamental stake in international stability. The case is somewhat more ambiguous with respect to China and Russia, which still favor more or less drastic alterations in the distribution of global power. But both are also cognizant of their limitations and aware of their interest in cooperating with the West. China is so inclined largely because it is an ongoing economic success; Russia because it is not. China thrives on foreign investment; Russia fears potential threats from its immediate south and east, and senses the diminished utility of its nuclear forces. China is self-confident; Russia is self-conscious.

Hence, both Russia and China may be susceptible to a strategy aimed at their inclusion in cooperative international structures. To

---

Reprinted with permission. "Living with Russia," *The National Interest* (Fall 2000).

that end, two Eurasian power triangles must be steadily managed and, over time, more directly connected: one involving the United States, the European Union and Russia; and the other involving the United States, Japan and China.[1] For that linkage to be effective, the constructive engagement of Russia is essential.

To be sure, neither America nor, even less, Europe can by itself seduce or transform Russia. Russia's epiphany must come from within, much as was the case earlier in the twentieth century with the collapse of the Ottoman Empire and the emergence of the modern Turkish state. But both America and Europe can help create not only a congenial but a compelling context for desirable change. And for that reason, despite justifiable short-term pessimism regarding the outlook of Russia's current political leadership, there is a reasonable basis for longer-term optimism.

THE HISTORICAL SETTING

The emergence of a democratic, Europe-oriented, post-imperial and national Russian state would provide historically relevant and strategically stabilizing answers to the two questions that haunt politically-minded Russians today: what is Russia, and where is Russia? These questions are being posed in an environment bordering on social catastrophe and in a context of geopolitical vulnerability.

One cannot underestimate the cumulative damage inflicted on the Russian people by seventy years of communism. Russia's current condition should not be judged by the superficial glitter of Moscow or St. Petersburg, the primary beneficiaries of Western financial inflows, or by occasional ups and downs in Russian growth rates. The painful reality is that the communist experiment has bequeathed to the Russian people a ruined agriculture, a retarded and in many places primitive social infrastructure, a backward economy increasingly facing the risk of progressive de-industrialization, a devastated environment, and a demographically threatened population.

To measure precisely the cumulative effects of that legacy is impossible. They are both massive and enduring. Russia's current crisis coincides with the collapse of the five hundred year-old Russian Empire, which had expanded in the Soviet era into an even larger communist empire. The domestic crisis threatens the well-being of the Russian people; the imperial collapse, while posing a potential geopolitical challenge, confuses, tempts and frustrates the country's political elite—an elite that for decades was not only doctrinally stupefied, but at times also lethally purged.[2] That elite grew accustomed to the privileges and satisfactions of Russia's global status, a status for which today there is no solid foundation.

The last ten years have compounded rather than resolved these challenges. Russia's relative openness has made the Russian people quite aware of the truly enormous gap separating their condition from that of their West European neighbors. The increasingly widespread awareness that a densely populated China next door is also doing incomparably better is an additional source of anxiety. Finally, for a state long accustomed to thinking of itself as America's principal rival, it is galling to contemplate the fact that Russia's GDP, measured in terms of purchasing power parity, is only about one-tenth of America's, roughly half of India's, and somewhat less than Brazil's.

It must also be troubling for informed Russians to learn that last year China benefited from more than $43 billion in direct foreign investment (bringing the 1992–99 total to about $350 billion)—and that the much smaller post-communist Poland was the beneficiary in 1999 alone of $8 billion in such investment—while only $2–$3 billion was directly invested from abroad in Russia during the same period (making for a meager total of $11.7 billion over 1992–99). Flagging foreign investment derives in part from Russia's poor international economic image. In the 1999 Global Competitiveness Report, Russia was ranked last among the 59 countries surveyed (China was 32, Zimbabwe 57, and Ukraine 58). In a comparative assessment of corruption in 99 states, Russia was placed at 82 (behind Armenia).

It is telling that there have been no major domestically funded investments in Russia over the last ten years. By 1997 overall capital investment in the production sector had fallen to about 17 percent of the 1990 level, and only lately has risen slightly. Moreover, it has been estimated that it would take roughly $25 trillion over the next 25 years to renew Russia's industrial infrastructure, which, on average, is three times older than that of the OECD countries. Indeed, even with sustained economic recovery proceeding at an annual rate of 5 percent, Russia would still account for only about 2 percent of the world's GDP by 2015. By contrast, the United States and the EU together will account for approximately 45–50 percent, and Japan and China combined for probably another 25 percent or so. The qualitative gaps in technological innovation and economic competitiveness between Russia and its western neighbors may be wider still.

The social picture is even bleaker. Some 70 million Russians live in urban areas affected by levels of pollution that exceed U.S. maximum contamination levels by a factor of five or more. About 75 percent of Russia's consumed water supply is polluted by U.S. standards. Russia's health system, long a source of pride, is malfunctioning, with many hospitals (especially in non-urbanized areas) lacking hot water and unable to meet even minimal hygienic standards. Some 100,000 cases of tuberculosis have been registered, and only about 40 percent of all recent births have resulted in fully healthy babies. According to one study, some 20 percent of Russian first graders have been diagnosed with some form of mental retardation. Male life expectancy has declined from approximately 64 years in 1990 to about 59 years in 1999 (alternative data suggests the figure might be about 61 years, still very low by Western standards). The *World Health Report 2000* on national health systems ranked Russia's at 130, barely ahead of Sudan's.

Indeed, Russia's population has dropped from 151 million in 1990 to about 146 million in 1999—with annual deaths in recent years exceeding births by slightly more than 50 percent (about 2 million deaths and 1.3 million births per annum). While economic recovery and an improvement in public health programs could eventually slow the steep population decline, some demographic studies anticipate that Russia's population could dip below 135 million by the year 2025. Then, too, many Russians are moving out of the exposed northern and far eastern extremities of Russia to the more secure central region west of the Urals, thereby reversing long-standing efforts to settle the sparsely populated northern and eastern peripheries.

Russia, then, is confronted by a menacing combination of demography and geography. Its far eastern neighbor, China, not only has a population of some 1.2 billion, but an economy that in GDP terms is already four times larger than Russia's. It is also no source of geopolitical reassurance for Russia that Japan's economy is about five times larger than its own; and that to the west an expanding European Union is taking shape, with an economy already approximately ten times the size of Russia's and a population of some 375 million. Moreover, the much more prosperous Europe is allied to the United States, which has a population twice that of Russia and a GDP more than ten times as large.

To the south prospects are, if anything, even more ominous. That area is currently organized into nine states inhabited almost exclusively by Muslims. Their combined population totals about 295 million, not counting the population of the Europe-oriented Turkey, which is about 65 million. An additional 20 million Muslims currently live within Russia's borders. At current birth rates, by the year 2025 the Islamic population living immediately to the south of Russia could number as high as 450 million (not counting the projected 85 million Turks).

It is probable that most of the neighboring Muslim countries will be economically weak, enhancing the likelihood that they will also be politically volatile. Their populations—composed in the main of the younger generation, which is restless, increasingly nationally self-conscious and more intensely Islamic in self-definition—could prove quite susceptible to extremist appeals. Unless handled with great skill and genuine moderation by their formerly imperial neighbor, their political awakening could acquire a fervent anti-Russian cast, of which the Russian mishandling of Chechnya might be only a harbinger.

Much, therefore, depends on the performance of the current Russian political elite—an elite that is strikingly different in composition and outlook from its post-communist counterparts in Central Europe. Russia's current leadership includes no former political dissidents, not even one. Moreover, in Central Europe the anti-Communist opposition—Solidarity in Poland, Sajudis in Lithuania, and Charter 77 in Prague—represented a critical mass that was subsequently capable of undertaking democratic reforms. In most Central European states, the Communist parties also quickly converted themselves into social-democratic ones, generally supportive of reforms and of closer ties with both NATO and the EU.

In contrast, the current Russian political elite is largely an alliance of former apparatchiki, criminalized oligarchs, and the KGB and military leadership. Their renunciation of the Soviet past has been perfunctory: the retention of a mausoleum in the middle of Moscow honoring the embalmed corpse of the founder of the gulag neatly encapsulates their mindset. Indeed, President Vladimir Putin's new team is composed of individuals who, with no exception, could now be serving in the higher echelons of the Soviet government (particularly the KGB) if the Soviet Union still existed. Putin's own political lineage is quite suggestive in that regard. He is a third-generation apparatchik: his father was a Party functionary, while his grandfather even served on Lenin's and then Stalin's personal security detail.

The present Kremlin leadership matured in the Soviet Union's waning years. By and large, it no longer believed in the crudities of Soviet ideology, but it relished Soviet power. The fall of the Soviet Union was for most of its members not only a historical shock but a calamity that could have been, and should have been, averted. While many of them dried their tears with profits derived from the kleptocratic dismantling of the state-owned economy, they nonetheless felt deprived by Russia's loss of international status. Putin captured their pent-up feelings at his inaugural when he spoke nostalgically of Russia as "a great, powerful and mighty state."

In rebuilding a Russia "which commands respect in the world," Putin's good tactical sense dictates that outright hostility to the West is to be avoided. Indeed, some accommodation with the United States is desirable, particularly in order to draw it into an anti-Islamic alliance in the event that Russia's problems in the south spin out of control. President Clinton's easy seduction into the anti-Chechen camp, in 1995 and again in 1999, offers a case in point. Russia's residual nuclear capability also provides the basis for a special dialogue with the United States, thereby enhancing Russia's prestige and perhaps even creating the impression of a special relationship.[3]

Russia's selective accommodation with the United States can be pursued in parallel with carefully calibrated efforts to cultivate anti-American sentiments in Western Europe, in order to dilute Western resolve regarding any further expansion of NATO and to exacerbate existing cleavages within the Euro-Atlantic community. Traditional diplomacy in dealings with Berlin and with Paris can also be exploited to fuel European rivalries, in order to impede the emergence of a politically more integrated EU, tied to NATO, on Russia's western frontiers. In any case, a détente with the West is the sine qua non of continued Russian access to needed Western financial assistance.

Above all, a breathing spell in relations with the West is needed if Russia is to achieve Putin's central goal: the restoration of a powerful Russian state. To the present rulers, the appearance of a dozen or so newly independent states following the Soviet Union's collapse is a historical aberration that should be gradually corrected as Russia recovers its power. Although it would appear that they realize that the end result may not be a single imperial state, they seem determined to attain the gradual subordination of the post-Soviet states within the framework of the Commonwealth of Independent States in a way that limits their practical sovereignty in the key areas of security and external economic relations.

That aspiration is the root cause of Moscow's vehement opposition to any Western economic presence in the space of the former Soviet Union. The Kremlin's attitude in this regard is still based on the old Leninist zero-sum approach: it is better for the non-Russian areas not to develop economically if such development entails a Western presence. That is why direct access of the newly independent states to the global economy through multiple pipelines from the Caspian Sea region is viewed by the current Russian elite with almost as much hostility as that shown toward Ukraine's flirtation with NATO. As one Russian Foreign Ministry official put it,

> The significant volume of funds already invested or planned by American companies for investment in Caspian oil business is defining a tendency toward a build-up of a political, and on its heels a military, U.S. presence in the Caucasus. In essence, without prior consent, the incorporation of the Caspian region into the sphere of 'the United States' vital interests' is taking place.[4]

Note particularly the quaint insinuation that Russia's "consent" is required for Western investment in the newly independent states.

Strategically, Russian policy toward what the Kremlin calls "the near abroad" has essentially three prongs. The first is to exercise pressure on both Georgia and Azerbaijan, increasing their vulnerability to eventual destabilization after their current presidents depart from the scene. Second, Ukraine's return to some sort of a special "Slavic" relationship with Moscow should be encouraged, with the Russo-Belarusian "union" providing a model of the "brotherly Slavic solidarity" to which Ukrainians should aspire. Third, pressure is to be applied to prevent the Baltic states from joining NATO, on the grounds that they were once "legally" a part of the Soviet Union.[5]

In brief, the Kremlin's current occupants believe that the "mighty" Russian state should be much more than a national state coexisting with others within the former Soviet space. Although most members of the current elite realize that economic recovery is a necessary precondition for regaining historical grandeur, some also place special emphasis on Russia's military power as the basis for its claim to global status. Not surprisingly, that view is strongly held within the top Russian military leadership and was explicitly reflected in the new military doctrine adopted in December 1999. Top military leaders are also particularly strong proponents of re-established Russian political power in a new "Eurasian union."[6]

It would appear, therefore, that the current elite is more preoccupied with the restoration of a dominant Russian state than with a historic reorientation of Russia. As a result, there is an obvious disconnect between the leadership's ends and the country's means. Contemporary Russia is simply too weak to sustain regional domination while nostalgically reclaiming superpower status. Despite numerous internal shortcomings, the new post-Soviet states are determined to retain their independence. It would take an enormous effort, far beyond Russia's present means, to subordinate them. Moreover, it is unlikely that the West, even were it inclined to accept some of Russia's regional aspirations as legitimate, would remain entirely passive if the independence of, say, Ukraine or Georgia—not to speak of the Baltic states—was threatened.

Further, Russian proponents of reliance on military power greatly underestimate the economically draining effects of any renewed arms

A Decalogue on Russia's Geopolitical Condition

1. Russia's economy is about one-tenth the size of America's, and its industrial plant is about three times older than the OECD average.
2. About 70 million Russians live in urban areas with levels of pollution 5 times higher than U.S. maximums, and about 75 percent of Russia's consumed water is contaminated.
3. Only about 40 percent of all recent births in Russia have resulted in fully healthy babies.
4. Russia's population has dropped from 151 million in 1990 to 146 million in 1999.
5. Russia's immediate neighbor to the east, China, has a total population of 1.2 billion; to the west, the EU has 375 million; and to the south live approximately 300 million Muslims.
6. China's economy is already four times larger than Russia's, while foreign investment in China during the last decade has been thirty times higher than in Russia. The EU's economy is ten times larger than Russia's.
7. Unlike post-communist Central Europe, the current Russian political elite is an alliance of the KGB-military leadership with former apparatchiki and criminalized oligarchs; all the current top Russian leaders could be serving in the Soviet government if the Soviet Union still existed.
8. The present Russian government has made it clear that its central goal is the restoration of Russia's power and not democratic reform.
9. Russia desires an accommodation with the West in order to gain a free hand in dealing with the new states in the former Soviet space.
10. Defiance of demography and geography could embroil Russia in conflicts menacing to its future as a major territorial state.

competition with America, and overestimate the political leverage that Russia can exercise through its essentially one-dimensional strategic capability. The fact is that Russia—already spending about 5 percent of its GDP on the military—cannot compete with the U.S.-pioneered revolution in military affairs. And while its nuclear weapons can serve as a deterrent, they are not an effective political tool; their value is gradually being diminished by nuclear proliferation, especially in Russia's immediate neighborhood.

A prolonged delay in providing realistic answers to the two questions that confront post-imperial Russia—What is Russia? Where is Russia?—could prove calamitous. Social mobilization on the basis of nationalism can only be a short-term remedy. Russia, underpopulated and socially deprived, could become entangled in flaming collisions with the Muslims in the south and more vulnerable to Chinese territorial encroachments in the east, while also antagonizing Europe (and America) to the west. An "alliance" with China would only subordinate Russia to China without solving its problems.

As a result, it may be only somewhat hyperbolic to suggest that the ultimate consequence of any prolonged failure to confront the full implications of Russia's menacing geopolitical context and of the debilitated state of its society could be the emergence not of "a Europe to the Urals" (as once envisaged by General de Gaulle), but eventually of a beleaguered and imploded Russia only to the Urals.

FOR STRATEGIC DIRECTION

In considering Western policy toward Russia, we would do well to reflect briefly on the collapse of the Ottoman Empire and the subsequent emergence of the Turkish national state. That experience is more pertinent to Russia's dilemmas than either Germany's and Japan's after 1945, or Great Britain's and France's after they ceased to be empires.

Unlike Germany and Japan, Russia was neither occupied and subjected to political "re-education" by the Cold War's victors, nor treated to large-scale social reconstruction under their direct supervision. For most Russians, the outcome was more ambiguous and confusing. Most at first did not feel defeated; many later felt deceived; few were receptive to Western tutelage.

Like the Russian Empire, the Ottoman Empire was territorially contiguous. Both Ottoman and Russian imperial elites drew many members from the subject nationalities. The boundaries of what was specifically Russian or Turkish territory were not very precise. In both cases, the empire was not a remote reality overseas but a seamless extension of the homeland itself. Hence, the sudden loss of empire was both more searing and directly disruptive.

In contrast to the efficiently repressive Soviet Russia, however, the long, slow decline of the Ottoman Empire spawned a significant minority of dissident intellectuals and young officers determined to model Turkey on the West European nation-states. The Young Turks, first organized in the late nineteenth century, gained increasing political influence, especially in the wake of the military defeats suffered by the Ottoman rulers. Some of them at first sought to re-create a modernized version of the old empire. But the defeat suffered in World War I prompted the next generation of reformist leaders, notably Kemal Pasha (who later became known as Atatürk), to embrace the concept of a modernized, post-imperial state, patterned on the European nation-states. In short order, the Swiss civil code, the Italian penal code and the German commercial code were adopted, and—very important to note—irredentist claims, derived from the imperial past, were explicitly renounced.

Three timely conclusions can be drawn from the emergence of the modern national Turkish state: first, Turkey would not be contending today for membership of the European Union were it not for the fact that Atatürk and his bold reformers represented a critical mass capable of effecting a psychological break with the past; second, this effort would not have endured if the West had continued to spurn Turkey; and, third, the process of historical self-redefinition is necessarily a prolonged one, to be measured in decades, not years, and is likely to be punctuated by periodic setbacks.

These conclusions contain important lessons for Russia. Although Putin displays a picture of Peter the Great in his office, his reliance on a KGB entourage and his professed admiration for his KGB predecessor,

Yuri Andropov, indicate that Putin is no Russian Atatürk. His geopolitical mindset reflects the thinking of the last Soviet generation and not of the first post-Soviet generation. Nonetheless, a new outlook is being nurtured beneath the existing political surface in the much more open conditions of post-Soviet Russia. And if only for actuarial reasons, the next generation of Russian leaders is unlikely to be the product either of the KGB or of the apparat.

That generation will come of age at a time when Russia's past imperial and global status will have become a distant memory rather than an entitlement. This inevitably will create a different global outlook. The next generation of leaders is much more likely to include graduates of Western universities and businessmen with genuine international (but not criminal) exposure, sharing a more widespread desire for Russia not only to be like the West but to be a part of the West. Not least, the Russian public will increasingly demand that its overall lifestyle begin to match at least that of Central Europe, and that Russians not be deprived of free access to the enlarging Europe next door. In short, a critical mass supportive of a genuine break with the past is taking shape.

To encourage that process, Western aid to Russia should be continued. But such assistance should not be directed to the central government. Russia is wealthy enough to be able to address its basic problems through its own resources, and Western aid has the tendency to perpetuate the worst inclinations in the current elite. Also, since financial aid is fungible, its diversion to military programs and operations (such as those in Chechnya) is a likelihood. Instead, Western aid should concentrate on helping Russia's nascent NGOs, which promote the emergence of a new, younger and more open-minded political elite—an elite that understands its own interest in a society based on the rule of law.[7]

The United States should also expand its ongoing visitor programs for younger Russian political and economic aspirants. In 1999 the Library of Congress initiated a program to bring to the United States some 2,000 younger Russian local officials for visits designed to acquaint them with the complexities of American democracy. This initiative deserves to be enlarged tenfold, and it should be complemented by a similar program for the newly independent states. After World

War II, tens of thousands of young Germans and Japanese were made familiar with American democracy, with an immensely beneficial impact. Younger Russians, especially from outside Moscow and St. Petersburg, should have the same opportunity.

However, the reorientation of Russia's outlook will be delayed if Russia's current political leadership gains the impression that its priorities can be successfully pursued, especially in the space of the former Soviet Union. That such illusions and nostalgia tend to be self-perpetuating makes it all the more important that Western policy both engage Russia and drive home the need for a basic redefinition of Russia's role in Eurasia. To facilitate Russia's historical transformation, Western support for the consolidation of the new states—especially Ukraine, Georgia, Azerbaijan and Uzbekistan—must be sustained.

Admittedly, the necessary strategic balance will not be easy to strike. In fact, some Russian sources have claimed that Clinton administration officials at times have encouraged Russian efforts to regain a dominant position in the former Soviet space.[8] Even the internationally condemned Russian assault on Chechnya did not produce a single noticeable U.S. response, on the grounds that it would be contrary to the policy of "engagement." It may unfortunately be the case that, during the latter phases of the Clinton administration, the one-sided U.S. emphasis on the West engaging Russia—but not on Russia engaging the West—could delay by some years the day when Russia comes fully to terms with its current historical condition.

To hasten rather than delay that moment, the transatlantic community must patiently keep the grand option of an ever widening and deepening association open to Russia, while persistently re-inforcing an environment that discourages any Russian efforts to turn back the geopolitical clock. Only then may the next generation of Russian leaders—no longer the products of the Soviet era and more likely to represent a new critical political mass—draw the sole realistic conclusion to the dangers posed by their country's internal malaise and external vulnerability: namely, that in order to recover Russia must opt for the West. What is more, Russia must do so unambiguously and unconditionally as a post-imperial state. Russia's imperial baggage cannot be dragged into Europe. Russia cannot be at once imperial and European.

A Decalogue of Strategic Guidelines

1. The lessons of the collapse of the Ottoman Empire are highly relevant to Russia's contemporary dilemmas.
2. Turkey's historic self-redefinition was made possible by the presence of a reformist critical mass and by the West's eventual responsiveness.
3. The next generation of Russian leaders may provide the critical mass needed for a decisive, post-imperial choice in favor of the West.
4. To that end, Western financial assistance should concentrate almost exclusively on the advancement of a new democratically-minded elite through the promotion of grassroots democracy and expanded visitor exchanges.
5. Propitiation of Putin's regime will only delay the desired evolution of Russia into a democratic, Europe-oriented, national Russian state.
6. Support for the newly independent states will help to advance the historical self-redefinition of Russia.
7. The EU and NATO should formally propose Russia's eventual association, and both the EU and NATO should explore with Russia specific initiatives to that end, including a special EU status for Kaliningrad.
8. In the meantime, both EU and NATO expansion should continue, thereby eliminating any geopolitical ambiguities or temptations in the areas immediately west of Russia.
9. A transcontinental security dialogue on strategic doctrine, building on a closer NATO-Russia connection, eventually could link the two key Eurasian security triangles.
10. Effective engagement cannot be pursued through one-sided courtship but only by shaping a decisive geopolitical context, in which a choice for the West becomes Russia's only viable option.

To prepare the ground for that historic choice, it is crucial that the West signal clearly that the continued enlargement of the EU and of NATO does not exclude a priori the possibility of Russia's eventual participation. Although President Clinton gave such a signal in his "Charlemagne" speech in Aachen in June 2000, he does not speak for the EU or even for NATO. A formal statement to that effect should be made, perhaps jointly by both organizations. Clearly, a truly democratic Russia that desires to be part of the West should have the option of becoming, in some mutually acceptable fashion, associated closely with both the EU and NATO. The precise modalities need not be spelled out now; in fact, given Russia's present condition and orientation, any effort to do so would be counterproductive. But the option should be held out.

In the meantime, a strategic setting favorable to that prospect should be fostered. Steps can be taken to enhance gradually the role of the Euro-Atlantic Partnership Council, which sponsors joint security programs between NATO states and Partnership for Peace members. While the United States in particular should be alert not to fall into the trap of becoming Russia's ally against the Muslims (or the Chinese), the serious possibility of conflicts spreading like grass fire throughout Central Asia might, over time, dilute Russia's hostility to greater Western involvement in the region. Moscow might then view more favorably not only greater economic access to the region, but also a larger role for peacekeeping by the Organization for Security and Co-operation in Europe (OSCE) and eventually perhaps even by NATO.

The EU's forthcoming expansion to Central Europe, even if somewhat delayed, is bound to include Poland and eventually the Baltic states. In that context, discussions with Russia regarding a possible special EU status for the Kaliningrad region could prove fruitful, not only resolving the region's persisting economic problems but also initiating closer EU-Russia arrangements. The same is true regarding the EU's ongoing efforts to promote Baltic regional cooperation that embrace both the St. Petersburg and Kaliningrad provinces of Russia.

In the meantime, President Clinton's initiative in inviting Russia to join both the EU and NATO has given greater urgency to the task of enlarging both. In fact, it is altogether unrealistic to contemplate

Russia's inclusion in either structure without Central Europe's full and prior inclusion. It is equally unrealistic, and even risky, to envisage delaying Central Europe's full membership until Russia either grants its permission or itself opts for Europe. That would be tantamount to granting Russia an indefinite veto, with the likely effect of stimulating the Kremlin's geopolitical aspirations regarding the Baltic states and Ukraine. The bottom line is that the consequence of any inclination to make NATO enlargement contingent on Russia's permission is a prescription for the perpetuation of geopolitical ambiguity on the western fringes of Russia, which will impede Russia's own internal evolution. Indeed, Russia's willingness to acquiesce to the further eastward expansion of NATO, particularly regarding the Baltic states, is a litmus test of the sincerity of any declared choice by Moscow in favor of a European and a transatlantic connection.

Constructive initiatives toward Russia thus will only be credible if they are matched by tangible steps toward the enlargement of both the EU and NATO. That dual enlargement is desirable in itself, and also because it eliminates the risk of a possible collision between competing notions of "europeanism" and "atlanticism." Moreover, several European countries immediately to the west of Russia—the Baltic states especially—want to be, and have the right to be, part of both the EU and of NATO. The next president of the United States should therefore urge our allies to move promptly on the admission of any democratic European state that meets the criteria for NATO membership, even before the year 2002 (the date previously set by NATO for the consideration of further enlargement).

The enlargement of NATO, in any case, has already proven beneficial for Europe's security, including Russia's. Most notably, it has made post-Cold War Europe more stable, anchoring Germany more solidly in its middle rather than making it a "border state," as some German leaders feared might happen after reunification. NATO enlargement has consolidated a sense of security among the new members and promoted better relations between them and their non-member neighbors. It has encouraged aspirant nations to improve their treatment of minorities and to settle their territorial disputes. It has also stimulated closer Polish-Ukrainian cooperation, reinforcing Ukraine's declared interest in its eventual association with the West. Last but not least, Romania and Bulgaria, because of their desire for membership, acted decisively during the Kosovo conflict to prevent the unilateral deployment of Russian paratroopers into Pristina—a deployment that could have precipitated a risky collision between Russia and NATO.[9]

The West should not be timid in affirming that Russia's acquiescence to the expansion of the EU and of NATO will hasten the day when Russia itself will be able to choose a more comprehensive association. Its precise form and extent will have to be negotiated, but a constructive Russian response should also prompt both NATO and the EU to begin a systematic review as to what kind of a shared security system, spanning "Vancouver to Vladivostok," might be both feasible and desirable. The enhancement of the OSCE, and its transformation from a "European" to a "Eurasian" framework, could likewise become timely; and NATO itself may eventually become a core element of a transcontinental security system.[10] Given a positive Russian attitude, it may not be too early to initiate informal exploratory discussions regarding these longer range prospects in the context of the NATO-Russia Joint Council, a step that would enhance the Council's significance and also gratify Moscow.

Thus, step by step, a linkage of the two critical global security triangles—involving the United States, the European Union and Russia; and the United States, China and Japan—may be constructed. That process may be hastened by the ongoing revolution in military technology, which raises the serious possibility that the more than forty year-old reliance on mutual deterrence may have to be fundamentally revised in favor of some form of strategic defense. Given that such a development bears directly on the immediate security interests of the three nuclear NATO powers, as well as of Russia and China, a comprehensive dialogue among them will become necessary beyond any bilateral U.S.-Russia discussions. That need will itself generate pressures for a standing Eurasian security forum.

It is important to reiterate that, while it should be the policy of the United States to engage Russia in an ever closer relationship with the West, such policy should not be confused with one-sided courtship.

Effective engagement should strive to create a geostrategic setting in which the Russian elite itself comes to realize that Russia's only option is its best option: to become genuinely "engaged" to the West.

It takes only a little imagination to conjure how beneficial it would be for Russia if one day the Kremlin startled the world by announcing that it welcomed the enlargement of the EU and NATO to include all those who wished to join, and that Russia itself hopes to qualify for membership of both. Such an epiphany would liberate Russia from its ominous geopolitical context and create favorable conditions for its acutely needed social rehabilitation.

The policy of effective engagement should be deliberately designed to make that choice Russia's only choice.

Notes

1. See chapter 1, "Living with China," and chapter 2, "Living with a New Europe."

2. Few in the West fully appreciate the scope of Stalin's purge of the social elite. In one chilling example from the Soviet archives, the NKVD's Moscow headquarters set quotas for the number of people to be immediately arrested and shot. That quota for Moscow in the fall of 1937 was 5,000; for Leningrad 4,000; for Vladivostok 2,000; for Sverdlovsk 4,000, etc. Subsequently, some of the NKVD regional offices submitted appeals, requesting *increases* in their quotas!

3. The current Russian leadership seems more skilled than its predecessors in influencing Western policymakers and opinion shapers, apparently relying more on the KGB's intelligence apparatus, those trained by the Soviet Institute on the U.S.A., easy access to Western centers of influence enjoyed by Russian oligarchs holding dual citizenship, and even on hired public relations firms. It stands to reason that the Russian leaders are not indifferent to the outcome of U.S. presidential elections and may be sensitive to the West's thirst for electoral campaign funds.

4. S. I. Chernyavskiy, "Washington's Caucasus Strategy," *Mezhdunarodnaya zhizn* (January 1999).

5. Disturbingly, the official position of Russia is that the Baltic states in 1940 gained "admission" to the USSR. See, for example, the official statement of the Russian Foreign Ministry, February 2, 2000.

6. A good example of such thinking is the doctoral dissertation of the influential head of the Defense Ministry's Main Directorate of International Military Cooperation, General Leonid Ivashov, titled "Evolution of Russia's Geopolitical Development" (May 2000).

7. For a compelling case for a much more discriminating Western aid policy toward Russia, see Michael McFaul, "Getting Russia Right," *Foreign Policy* (Winter 1999-2000), pp. 65–7.

8. "Off the record, State Department officials often talk unequivocally in favor of a Russian sphere of influence in Eurasia." Andrei Kortunov, "The U.S. and Russia: A Virtual Partnership," *Comparative Strategy* (October-December 1996), p. 347.

9. See Zbigniew Brzezinski and Christopher Swift, "Russia and the Kosovo Crisis" (Washington, D.C.: CSIS, October 1999), pp. 14–16, 19.

10. The case for the further expansion of the EU was made in chapter 2. On expanding the OSCE from a European to a Eurasian organization, see chapter 1. It should also be noted that the EU has initiated strategic consideration of a long-term security relationship with Russia, through its "Common Strategy of the European Union on Russia" of June 4, 1999.

Geopolitical Realities

What China Is and Is Not

1. China is neither an international adversary nor a strategic partner of the United States, though it is hostile to perceived U.S. "hegemony."
2. China is not going to become a global power, though it is a regional power capable of asserting its national interests.
3. China is not a direct security threat to the United States.
4. China does not pose a global ideological challenge to the United States.
5. China is not regionally destabilizing and is in fact behaving internationally in a relatively responsible fashion.
6. China is neither totalitarian nor democratic politically but an oligarchic-bureaucratic dictatorship.
7. China is not in compliance with universal standards of human rights and of tolerance for minorities in places such as Tibet or Xinjiang.
8. China is evolving economically in a desirable direction.
9. China is not likely to avoid serious domestic political strains because commercial communism is an oxymoron.
10. China does not have a clear vision of its political evolution or of its international role.

European Developments and Prospects

1. For most Europeans, "Europe" is not an object of personal affection. It is more a convenience than a conviction.
2. On the global scene, the EU will not be like America but more like a Switzerland writ large.
3. Most Europeans do not partake of anti-Americanism as the impulse for unity.
4. Integration is essentially a bureaucratic process and not the same as unification.
5. The EU's expansion inevitably collides with deepening integration.
6. The EU needs to expand for demographic and economic reasons.
7. A federated inner core of foreign-policymaking states within a larger EU of 21 or more states is not politically workable.
8. Slow expansion plus bureaucratic integration is likely to produce a Europe united economically but only confederated politically.
9. The EU is unlikely to acquire an autonomous military capability.
10. The EU will thus be a novel type of polity, with its global influence primarily economic and financial.

Russia's Geopolitical Condition

1. Russia's economy is about one-tenth the size of America's, and its industrial plant is about 3 times older than the OECD average.
2. About 70 million Russians live in urban areas with pollution levels 5 times higher than U.S. maximums; about 75 percent of Russia's consumed water is contaminated.
3. Only about 40 percent of all recent births in Russia have resulted in fully healthy babies.
4. Russia's population has dropped from 151 million in 1990 to 146 million in 1999.
5. To the east, China has a population of 1.2 billion; to the west, the EU has 375 million; to the south live approximately 300 million Muslims.
6. China's economy is already 4 times larger than Russia's, while foreign investment in China during the last decade has been 30 times higher than in Russia. The EU's economy is 10 times larger than Russia's.
7. Unlike post-communist Central Europe, Russia's current political elite is an alliance of the KGB-military leadership with former apparatchiki and criminalized oligarchs; all current top Russian leaders could be serving in the Soviet government if the Soviet Union still existed.
8. The present Russian government has made clear that its central goal is the restoration of Russia's power and not democratic reform.
9. Russia desires an accommodation with the West in order to gain a free hand in dealing with the new states in the former Soviet space.
10. Defiance of demography and geography could embroil Russia in conflicts menacing to its future as a major territorial state.

74 THE GEOSTRATEGIC TRIAD

Strategic Priorities

Guidelines for U.S.–China Relations

1. The future orientation of China, and not the future of Taiwan, should be America's central strategic concern.
2. An anti-Chinese defense arrangement with Taiwan should not be indirectly revived, and U.S. arms sales should be carefully calibrated in relation to the state of U.S.-China relations and PRC capabilities.
3. Peaceful reunification can be promoted only by a democratizing and increasingly prosperous PRC on the basis of a "one country, several systems" formula.
4. Respect for human rights in China should be fostered by a policy of indirection focused on the benefits of the rule of law.
5. The U.S.-China-Japan relationship is highly interactive, in a manner reminiscent of the U.S.-European-Soviet relationship.
6. The United States should promote a trilateral strategic dialogue with China and Japan regarding the security of Eurasia.
7. A pre-emptive anti-Chinese defense coalition, based on TMD, could become a self-fulfilling prophecy of a hostile China.
8. The OSCE should be expanded to include Asia, following five-way security talks involving the United States, Europe, Russia, China and Japan.
9. The G-8 should be enlarged to G-9 by the inclusion of the PRC.
10. The ultimate U.S. goal should be a China that evolves into a genuinely vested partner in an increasingly cooperative Eurasian system.

Guidelines for Transatlantic Relations

1. Europe remains America's natural and pre-eminent ally.
2. An Atlanticist Europe is essential to a stable Eurasian equilibrium.
3. An autonomous European defense capability, in any case unlikely in the near future, should not be opposed by the United States.
4. Allied political unity is more important than the enhancement of NATO's capabilities.
5. The United States should defer any deployment decision regarding a ballistic missile defense system until consensus is reached with NATO allies.
6. The United States should seek an enlarged NATO in Europe but not an "out of area" NATO.
7. The United States has a bigger stake in Europe's enlargement than in Europe's integration.
8. NATO and the EU should work together on joint plans for further expansion.
9. Eventually, Turkey, Cyprus and Israel might be included in both entities.
10. There should be no a priori limitations or exclusions on NATO and EU memberships.

Guidelines for U.S. Russia Policy

1. The lessons of the collapse of the Ottoman Empire are highly relevant to Russia's contemporary dilemmas.
2. Turkey's historic self-redefinition was made possible by the presence of a reformist critical mass and by the West's eventual responsiveness.
3. The next generation of Russian leaders may provide the critical mass needed for a decisive, post-imperial choice in favor of the West.
4. To that end, Western financial assistance should concentrate almost exclusively on the advancement of a new democratically-minded elite through the promotion of grassroots democracy and expanded visitor exchanges.
5. Propitiation of Putin's regime will only delay the desired evolution of Russia into a democratic, Europe-oriented, national Russian state.
6. Support for the newly independent states will help to advance the historical self-redefinition of Russia.
7. The EU and NATO should formally propose Russia's eventual association, and both the EU and NATO should explore with Russia specific initiatives to that end, including a special EU status for Kaliningrad.
8. In the meantime, both EU and NATO expansion should continue, thereby eliminating any geopolitical ambiguities or temptations in the areas immediately west of Russia.
9. A transcontinental security dialogue on strategic doctrine, building on a closer NATO-Russia connection, eventually could link the two key Eurasian security triangles.
10. Effective engagement cannot be pursued through one-sided courtship but only by shaping a decisive geopolitical context, in which a choice for the West becomes Russia's only viable option.

ABOUT THE AUTHOR

Zbigniew Brzezinski is a counselor at CSIS and a former national security adviser to the president. His many books include *The Grand Chessboard: American Primacy and Its Geostrategic Imperatives* (BasicBooks, 1997) and *The Grand Failure: The Birth and Death of Communism in the Twentieth Century* (Scribner, 1989).